Geometrix Seven

LOUISE ATHERTON

Testing – Use this page to test your writing implements and color palettes.

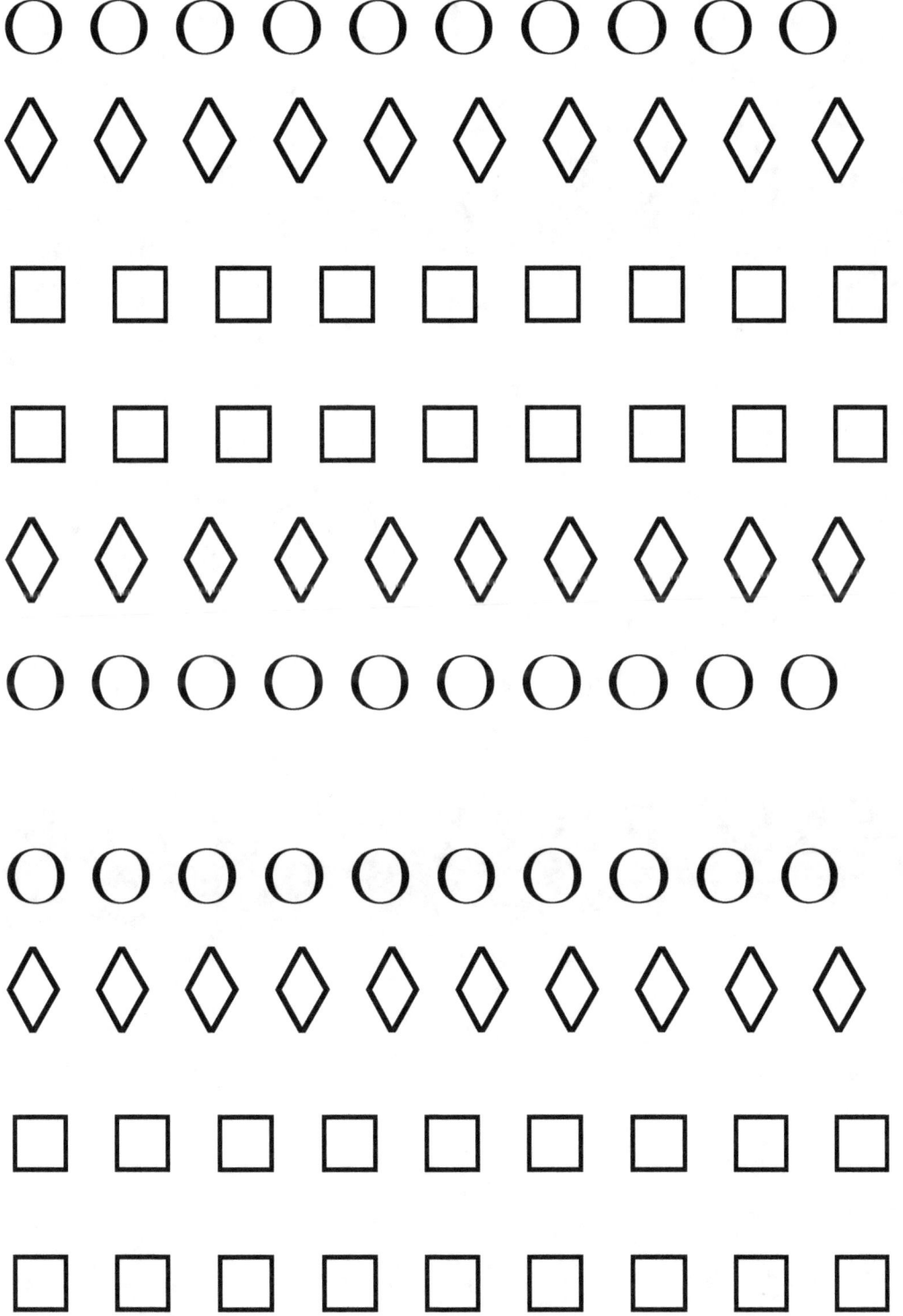

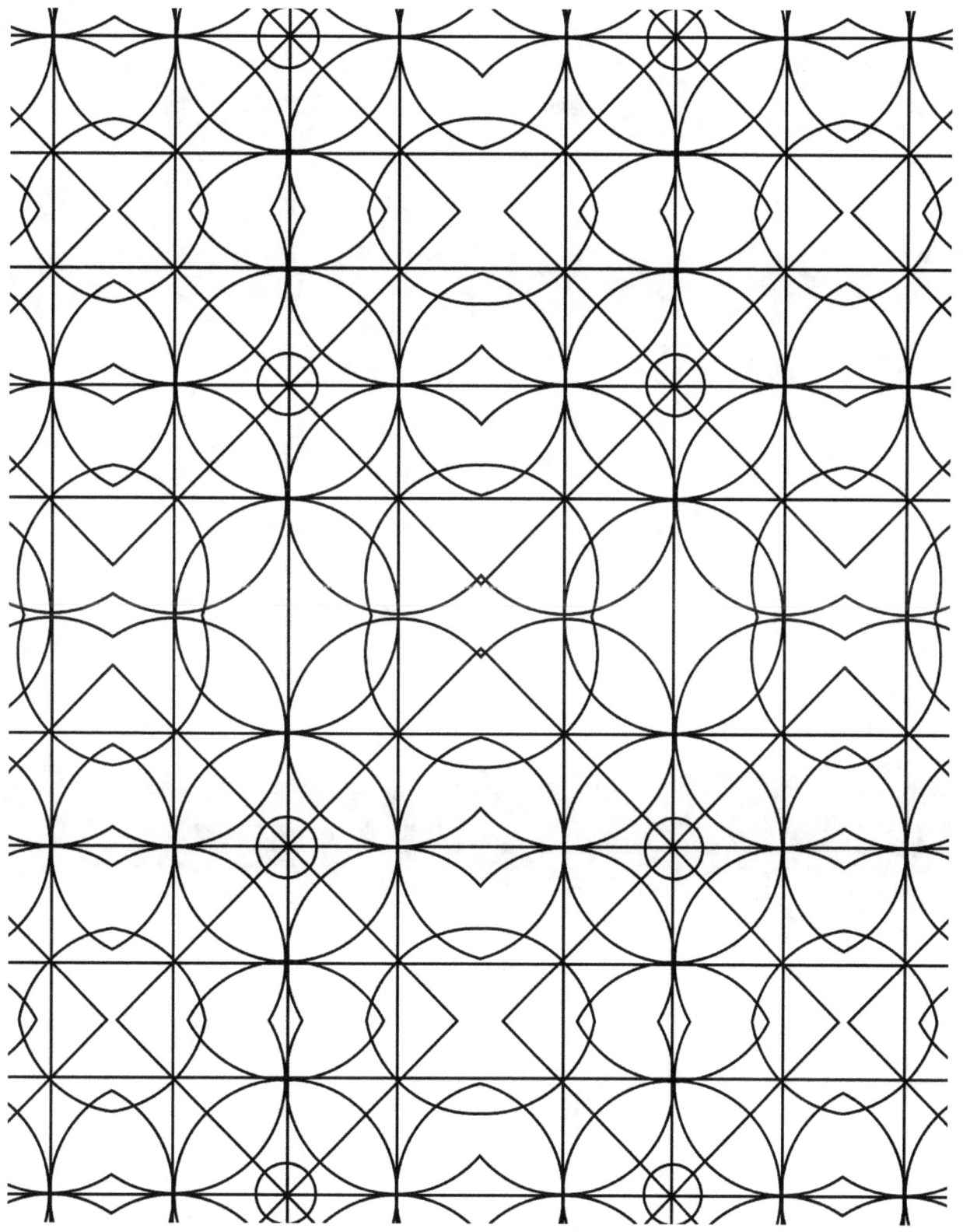

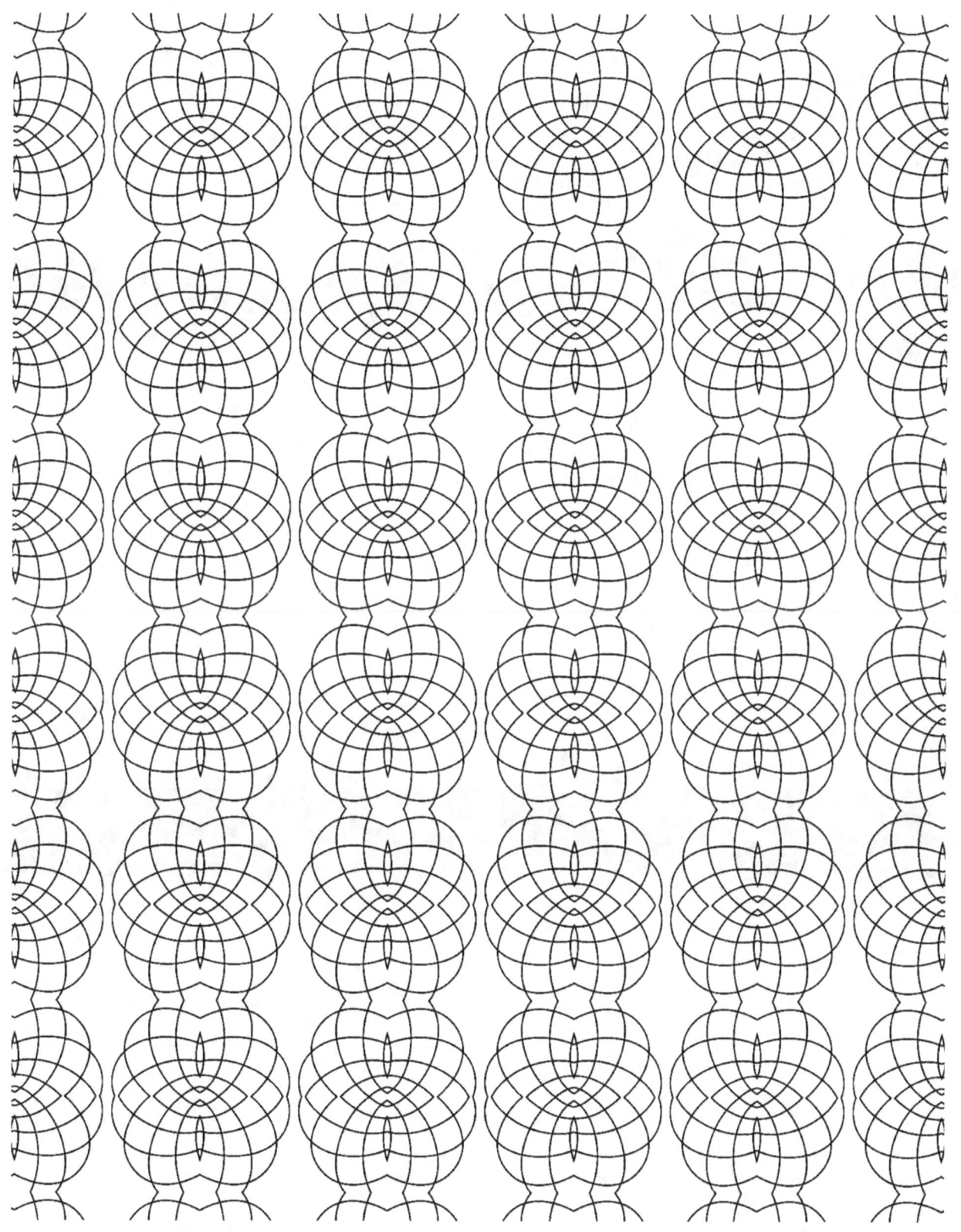

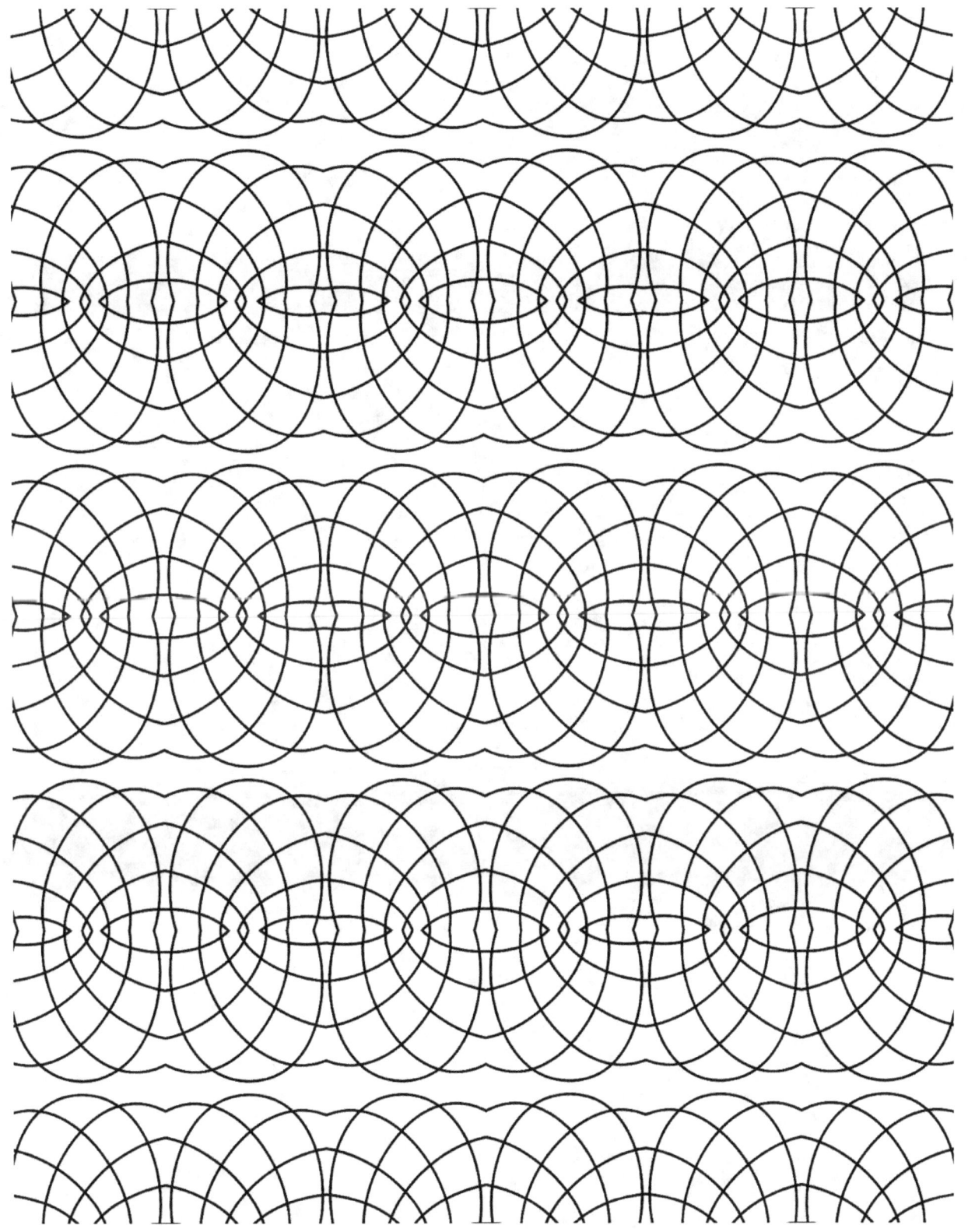

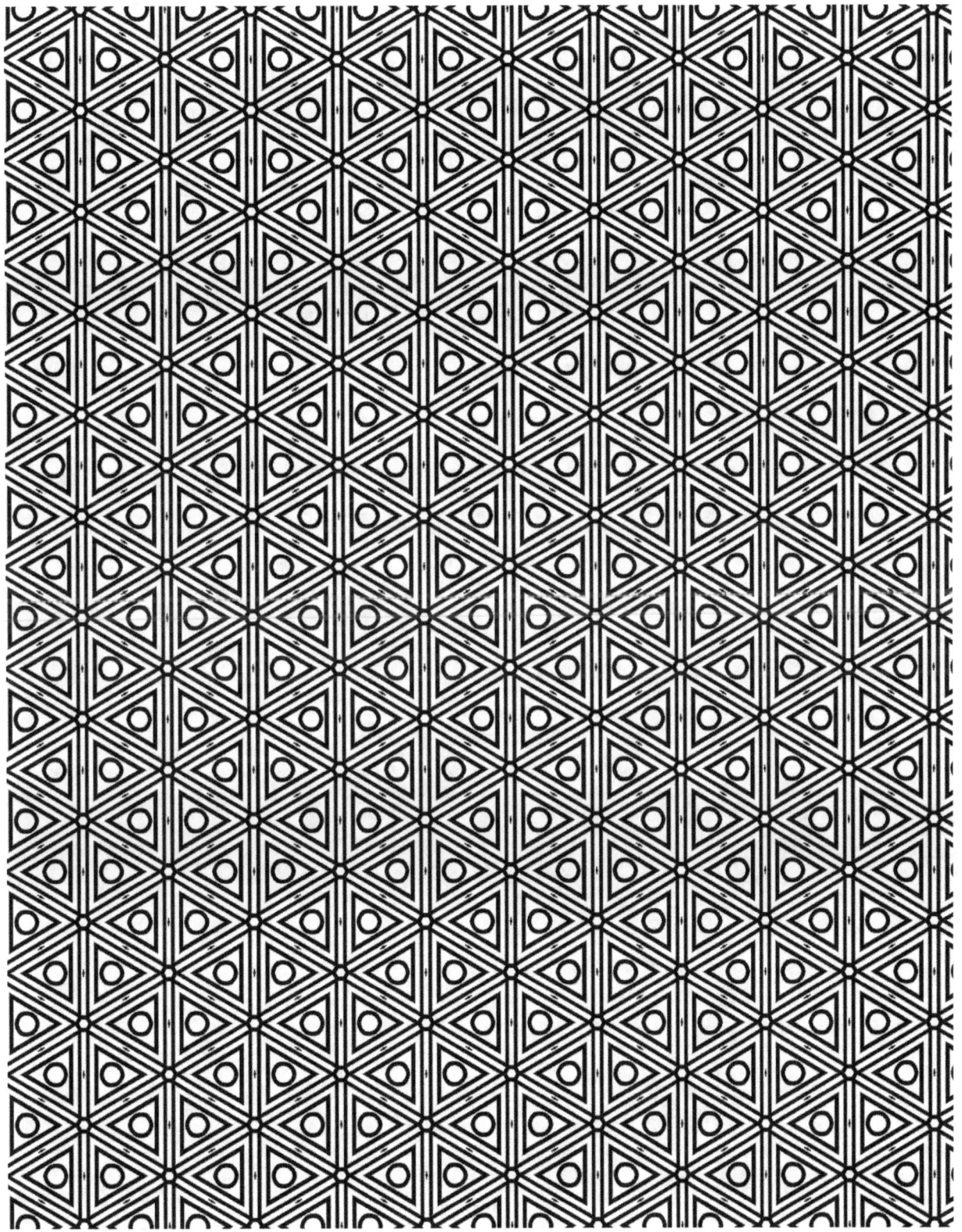

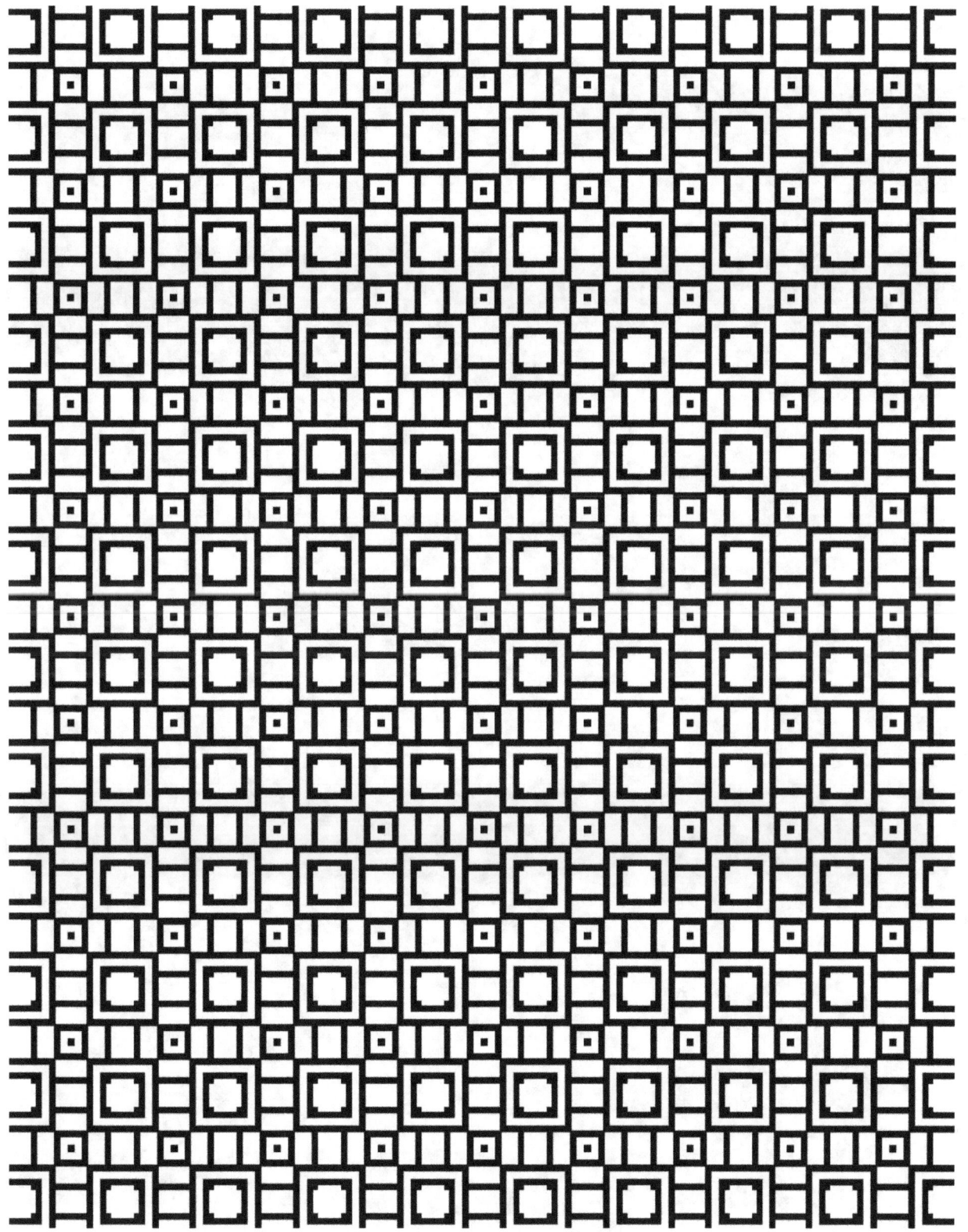

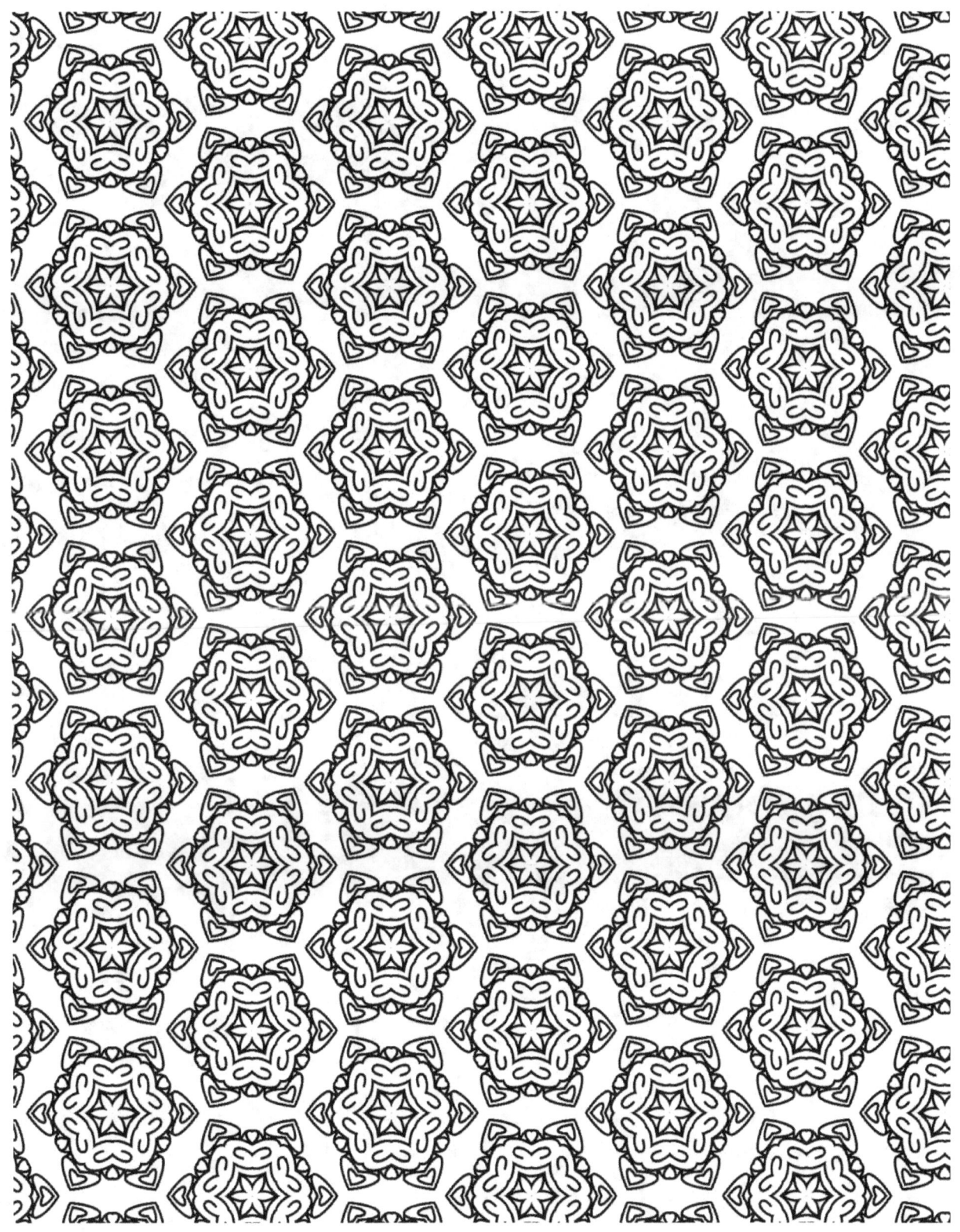

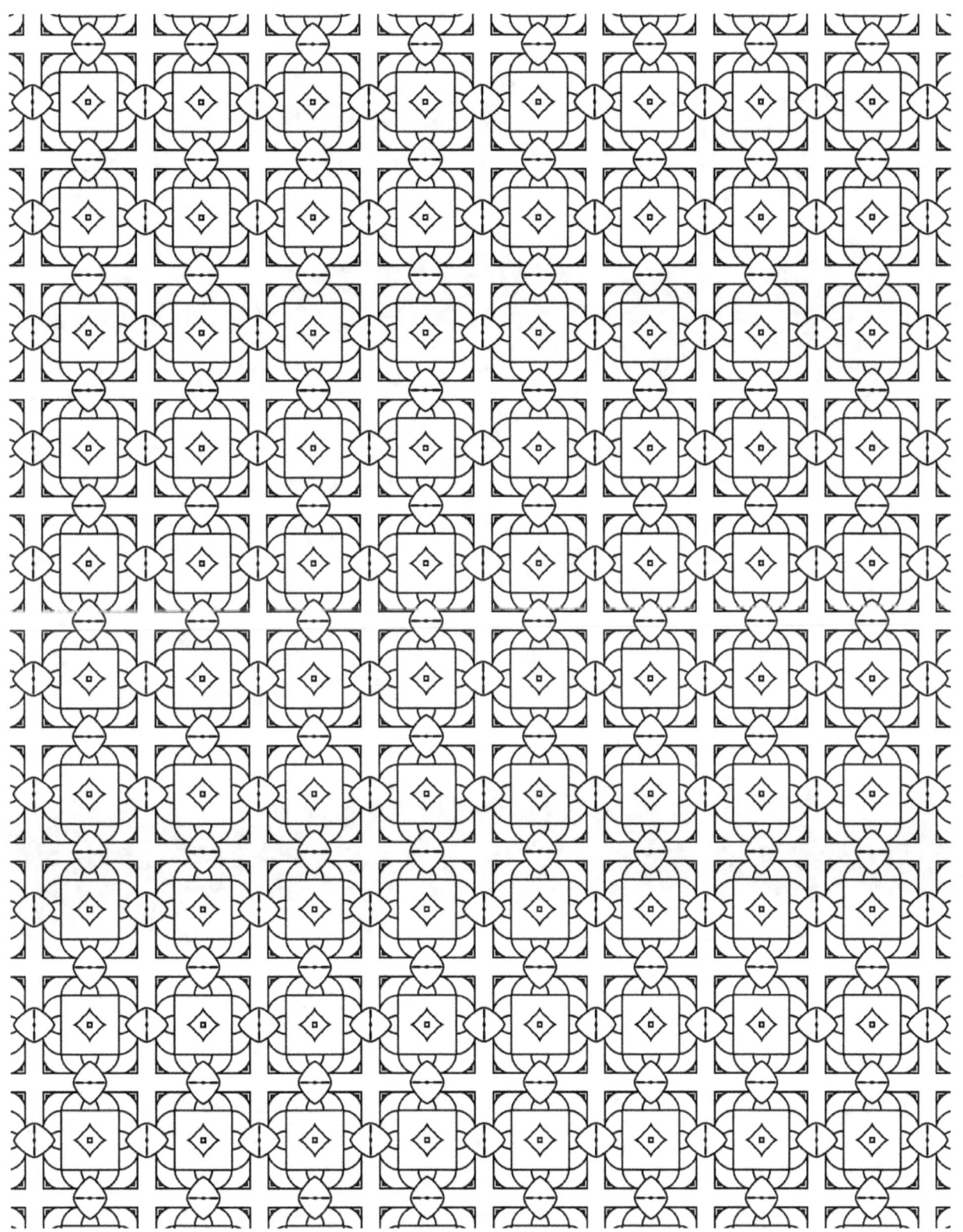

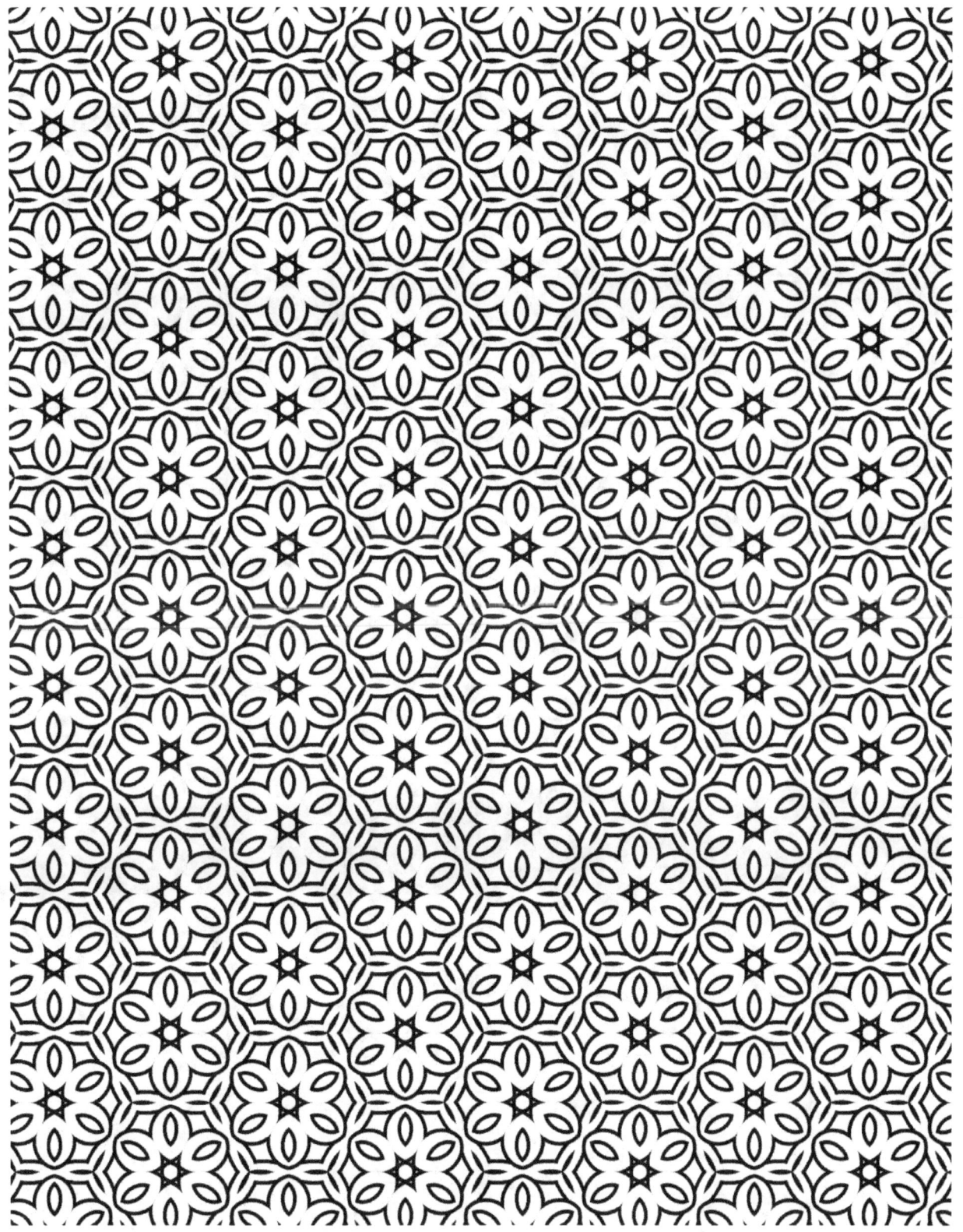

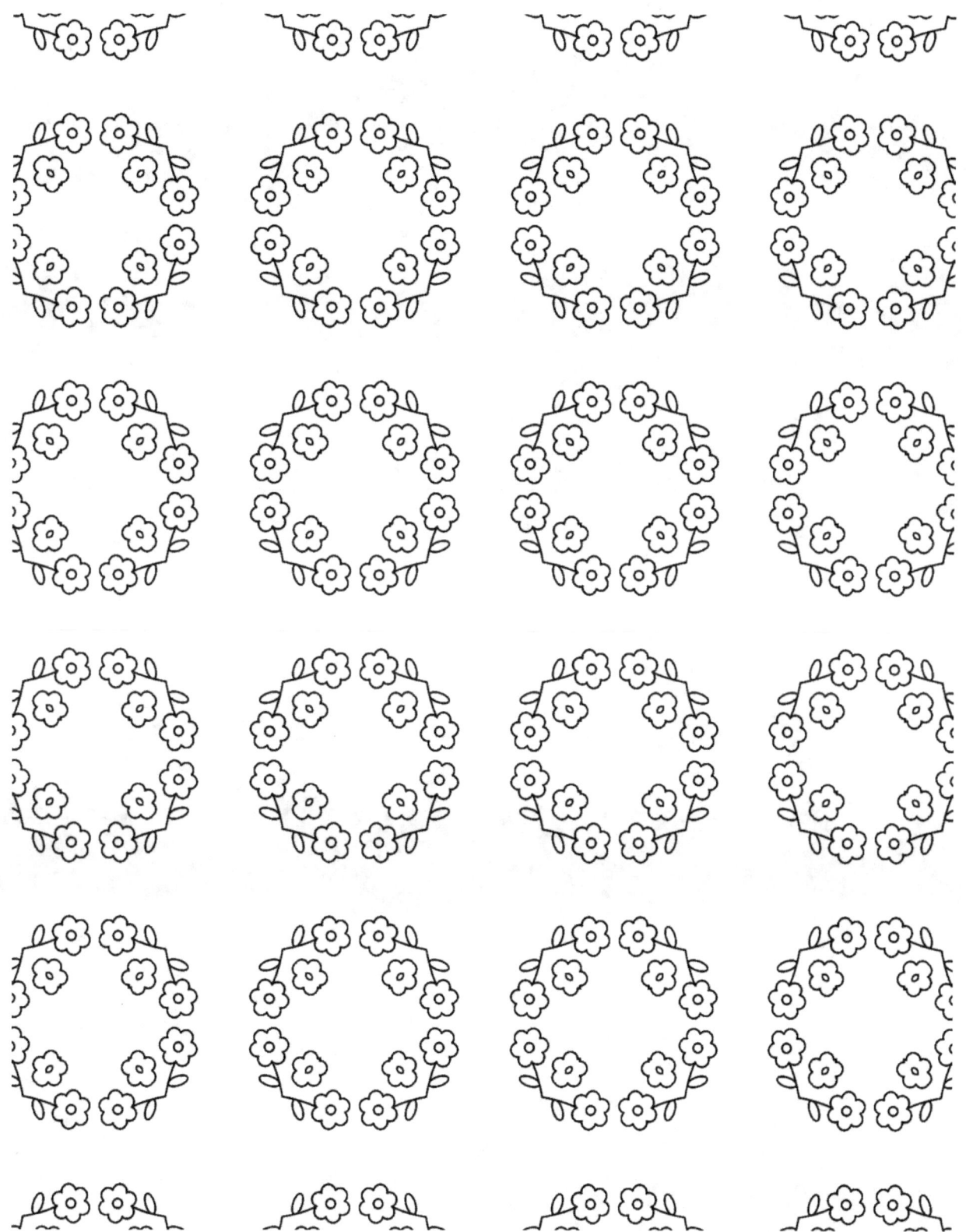

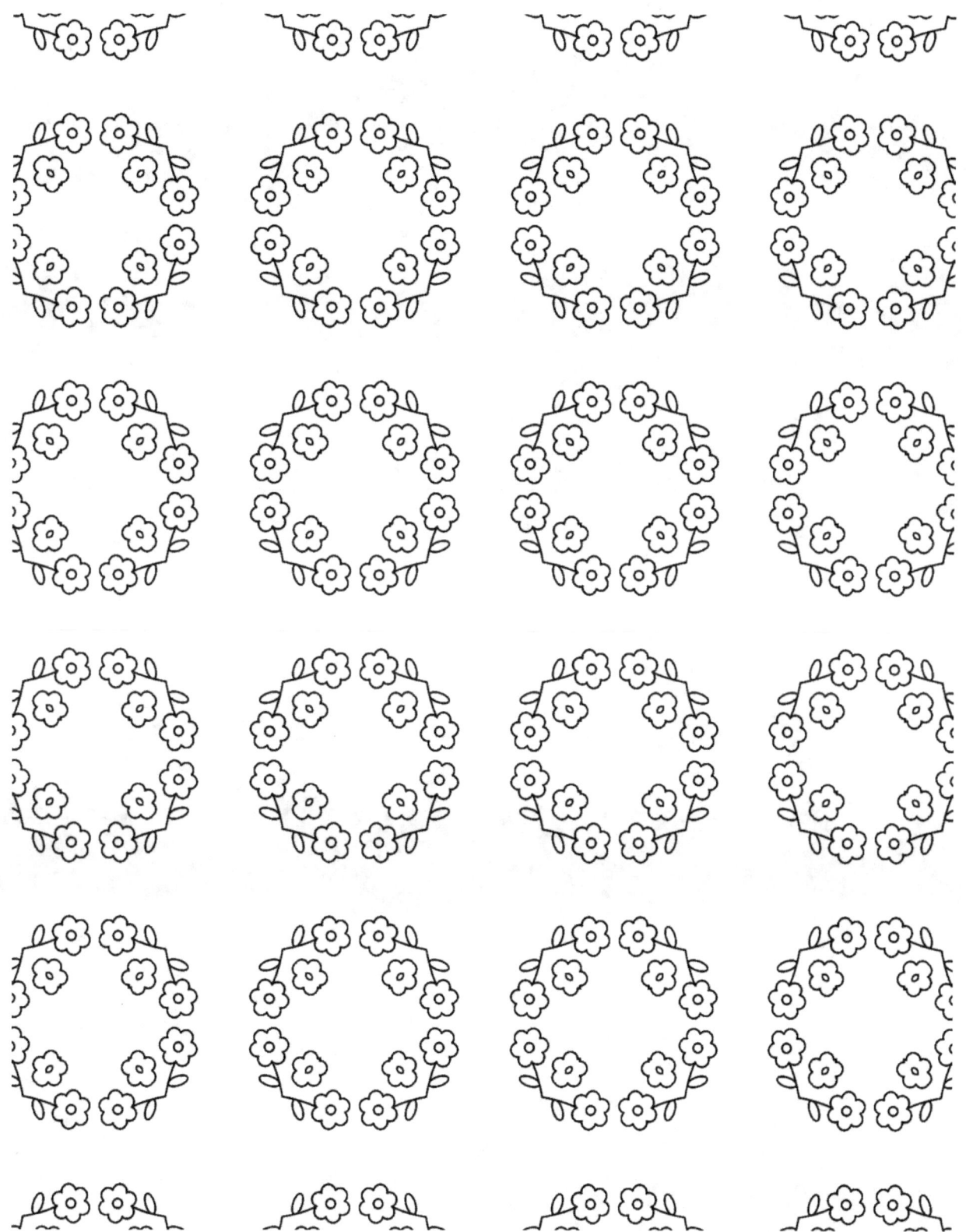

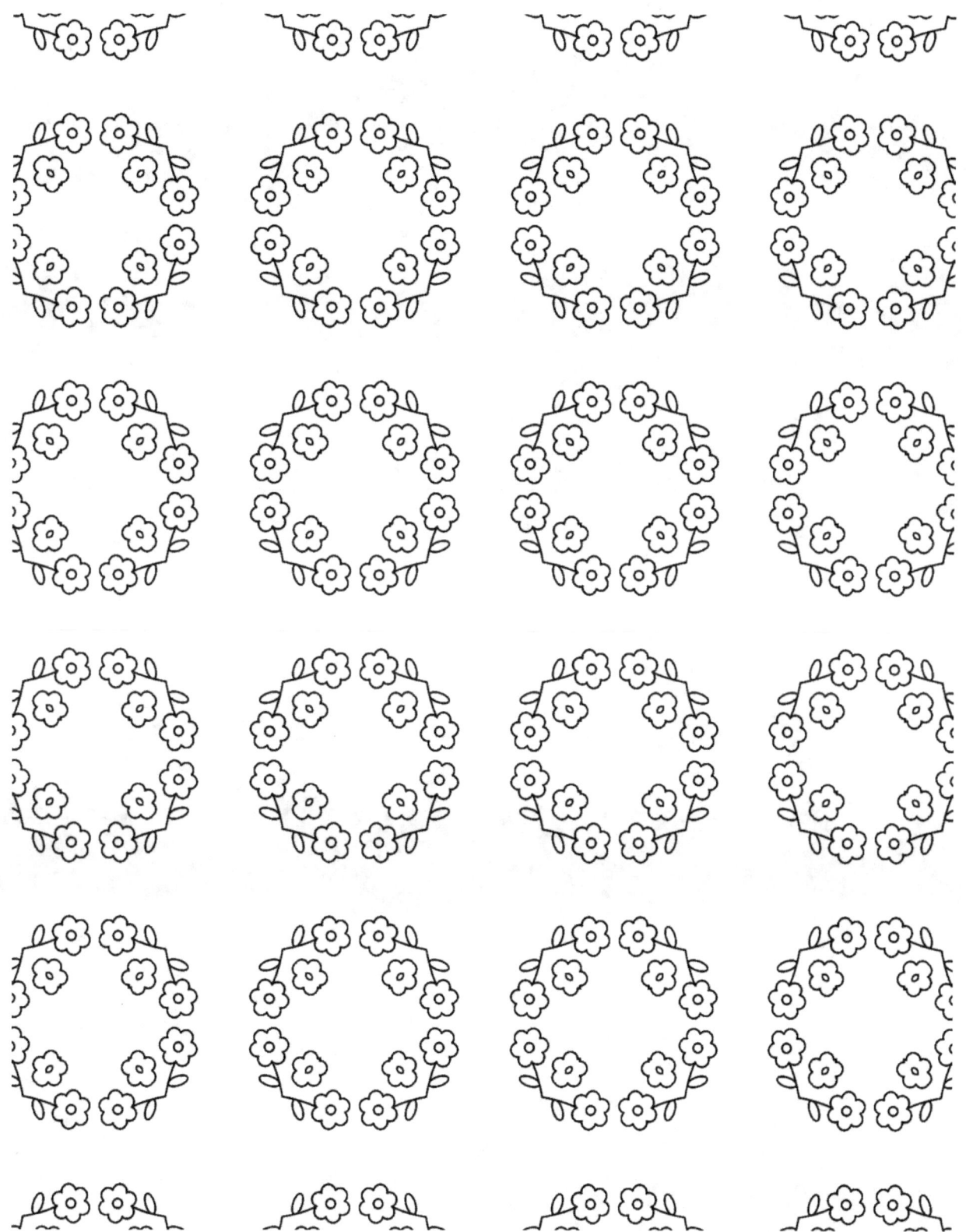

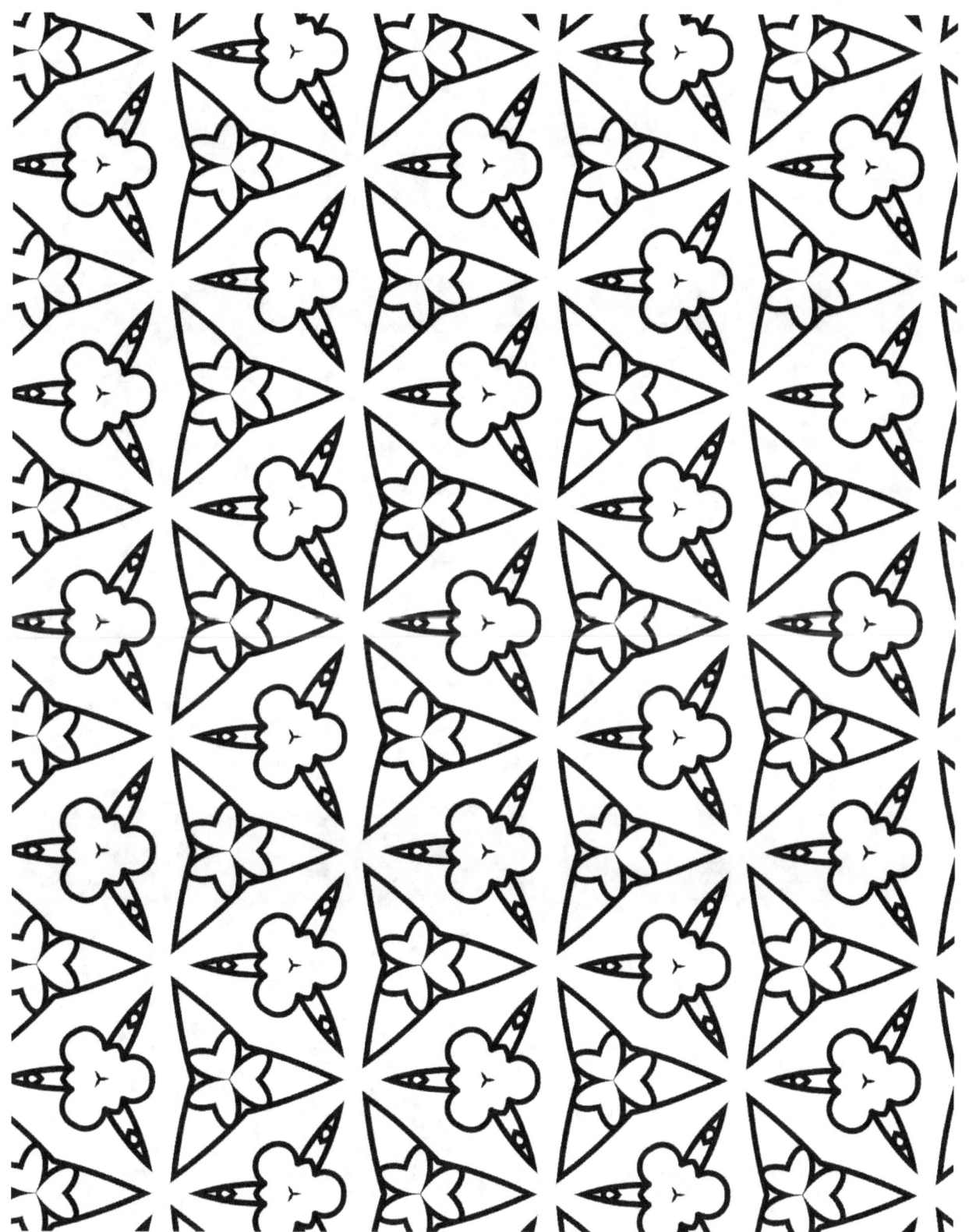

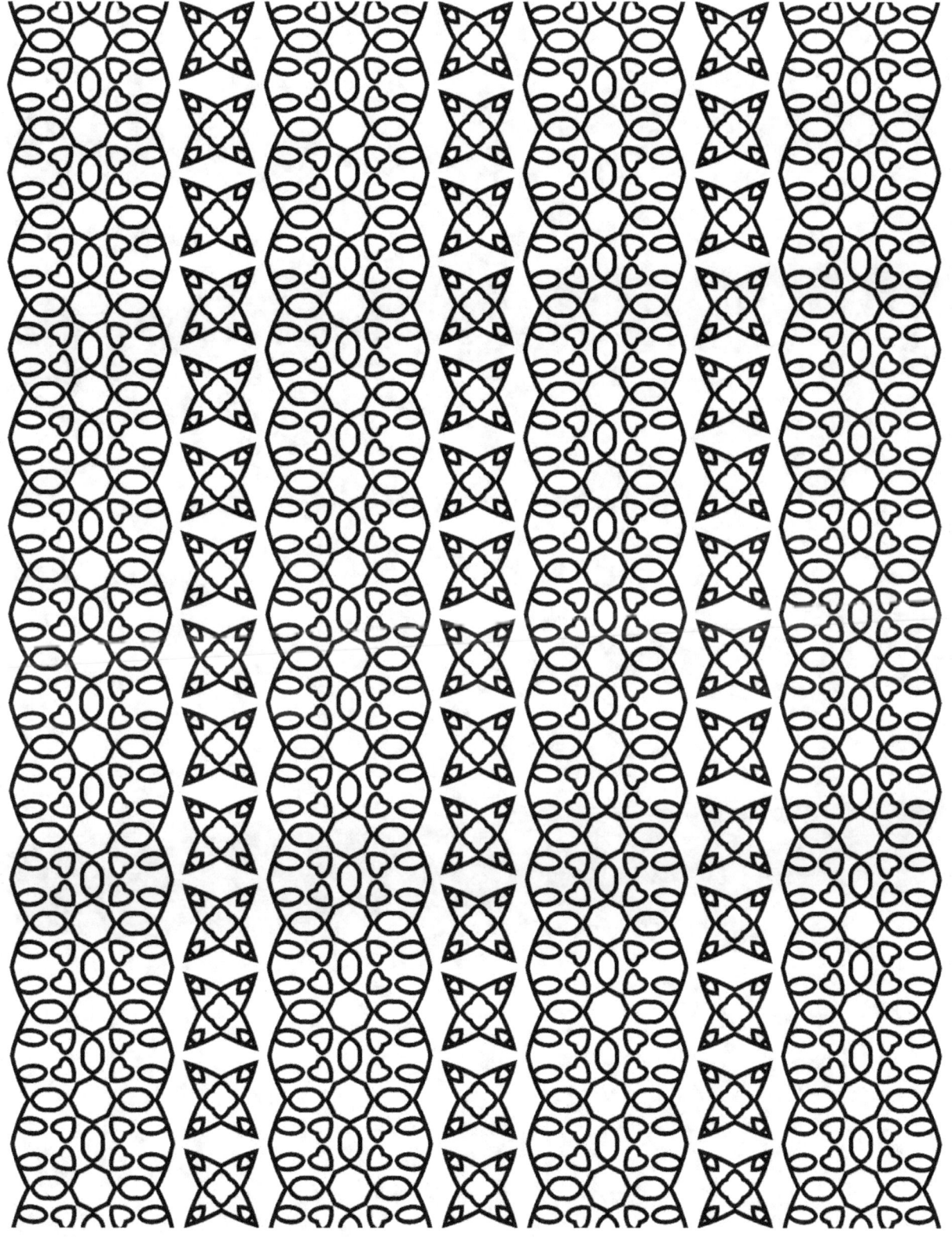

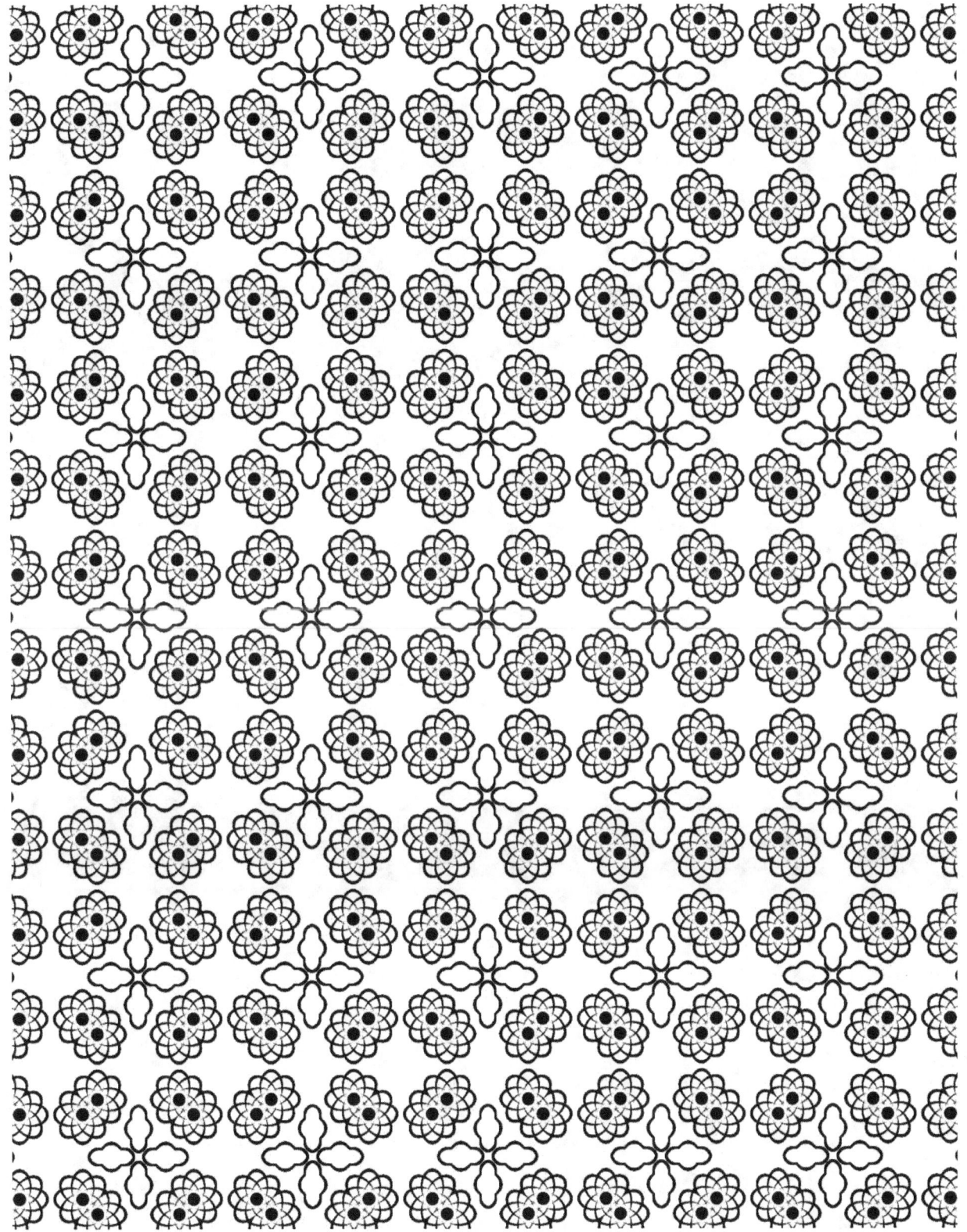

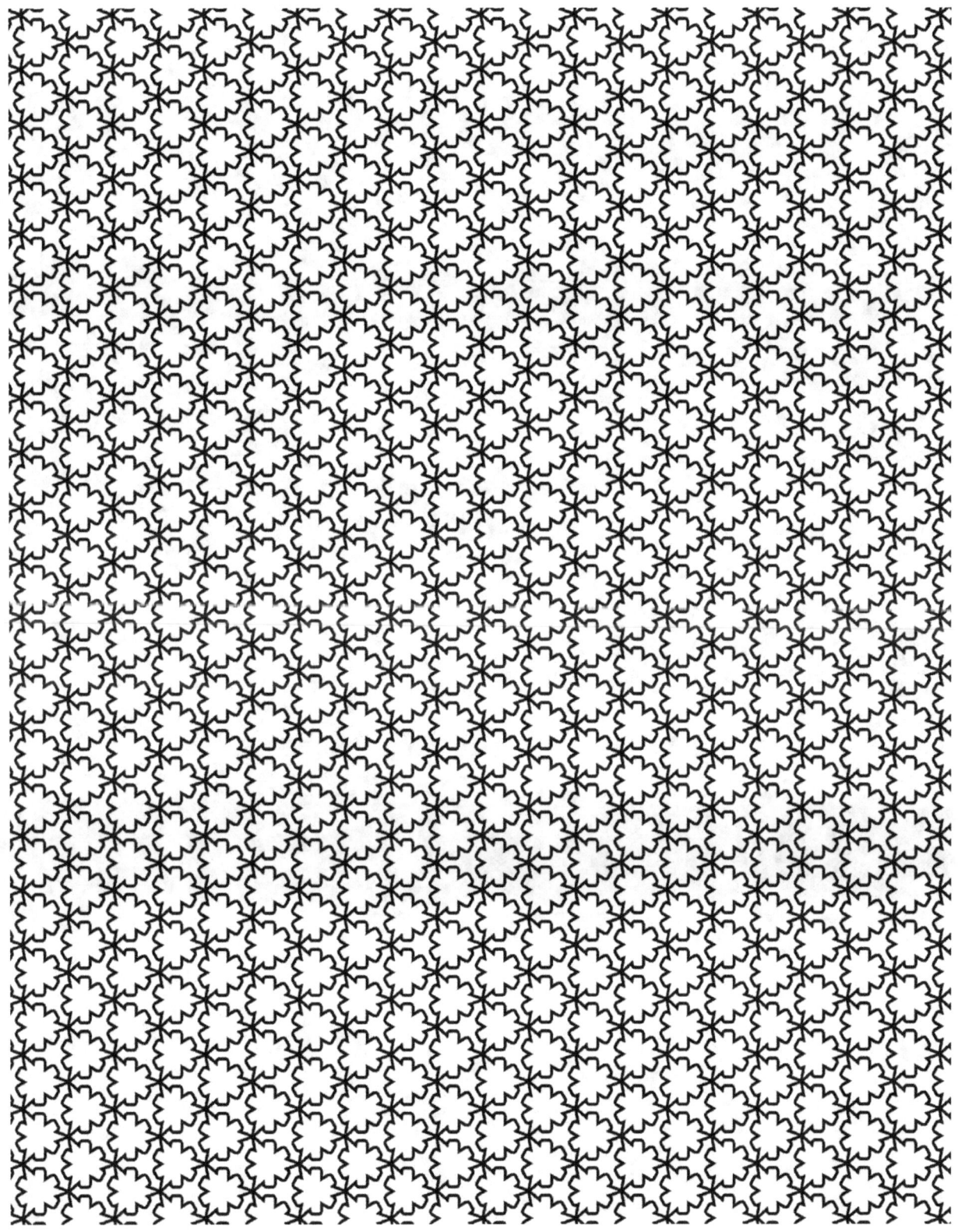

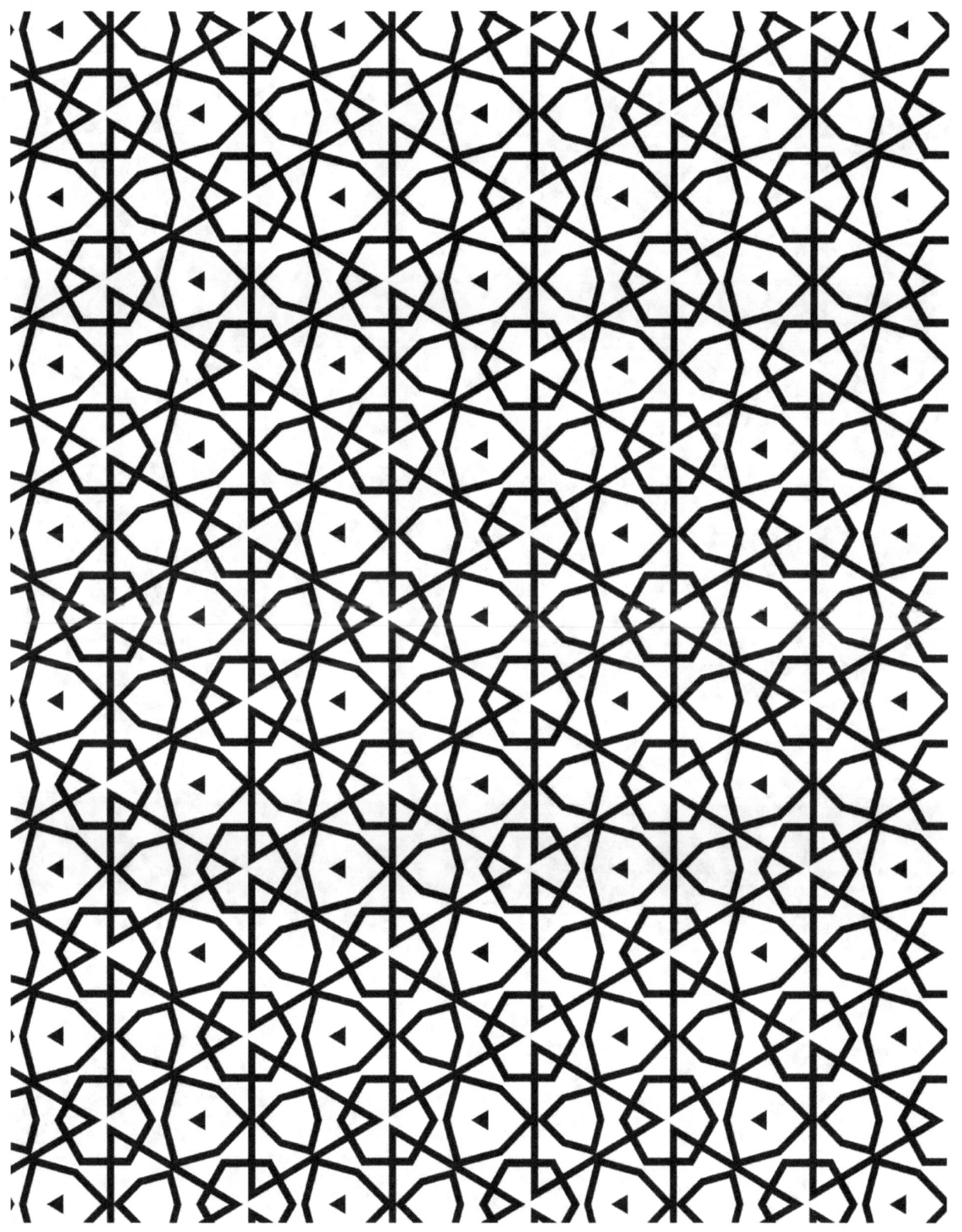

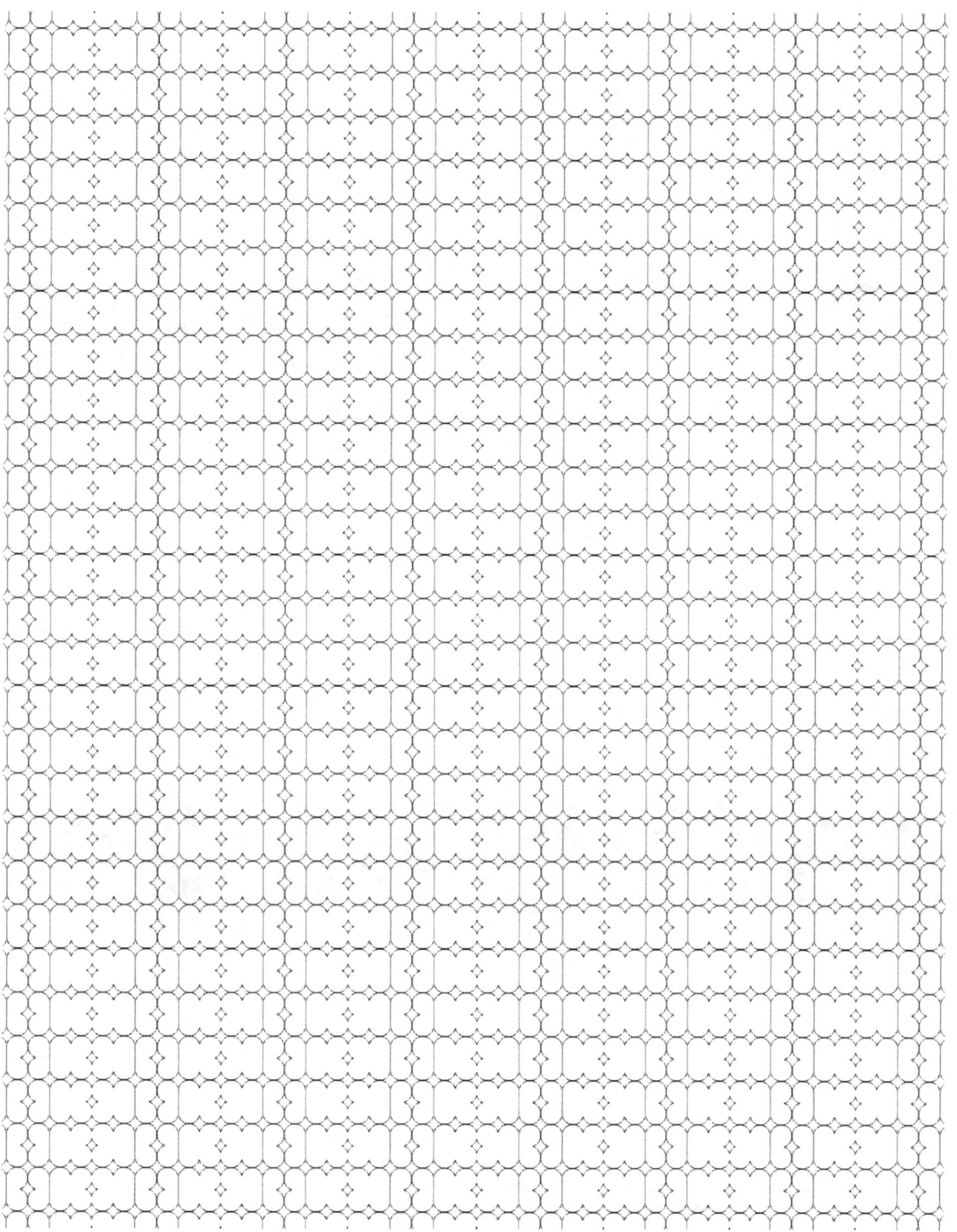

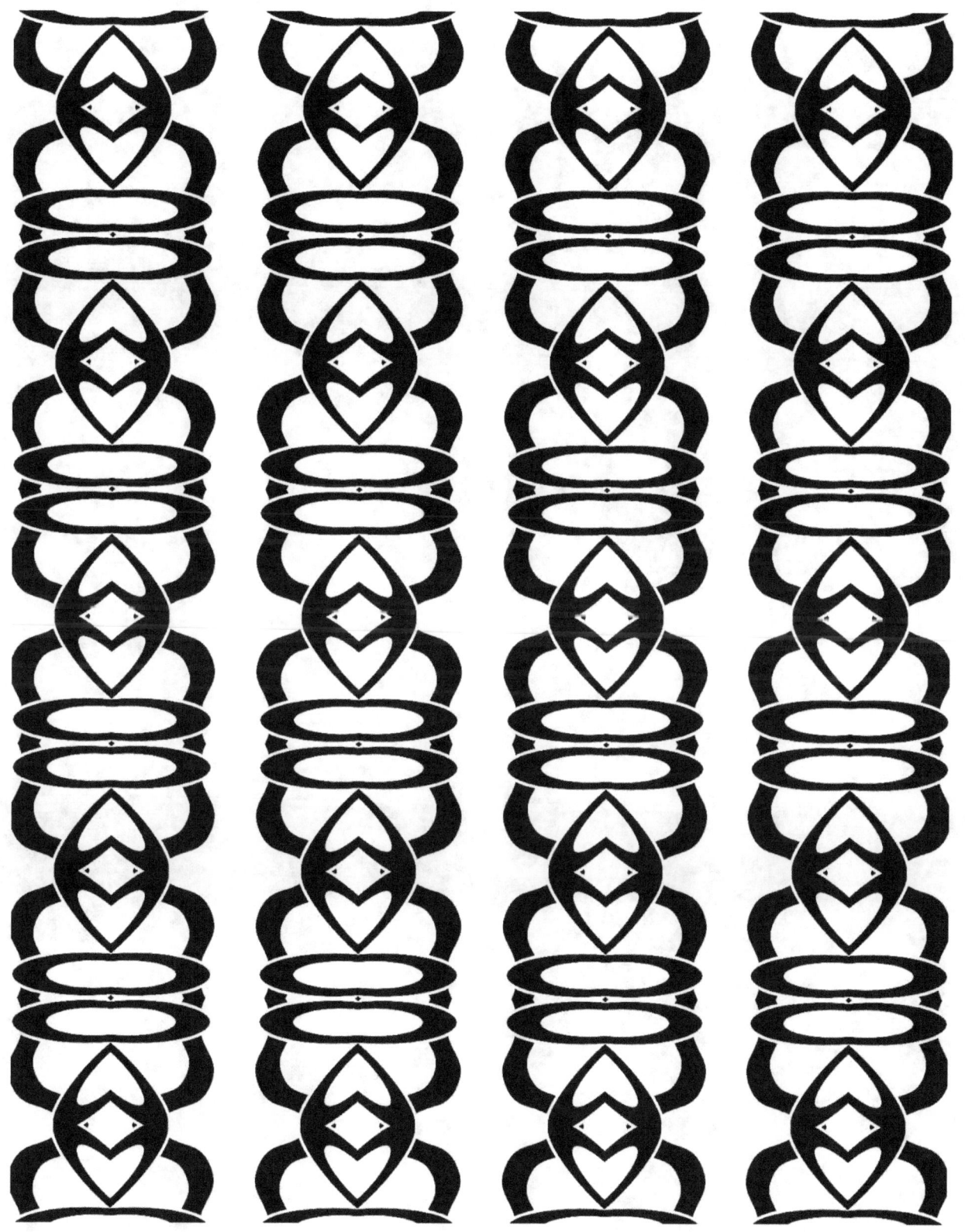

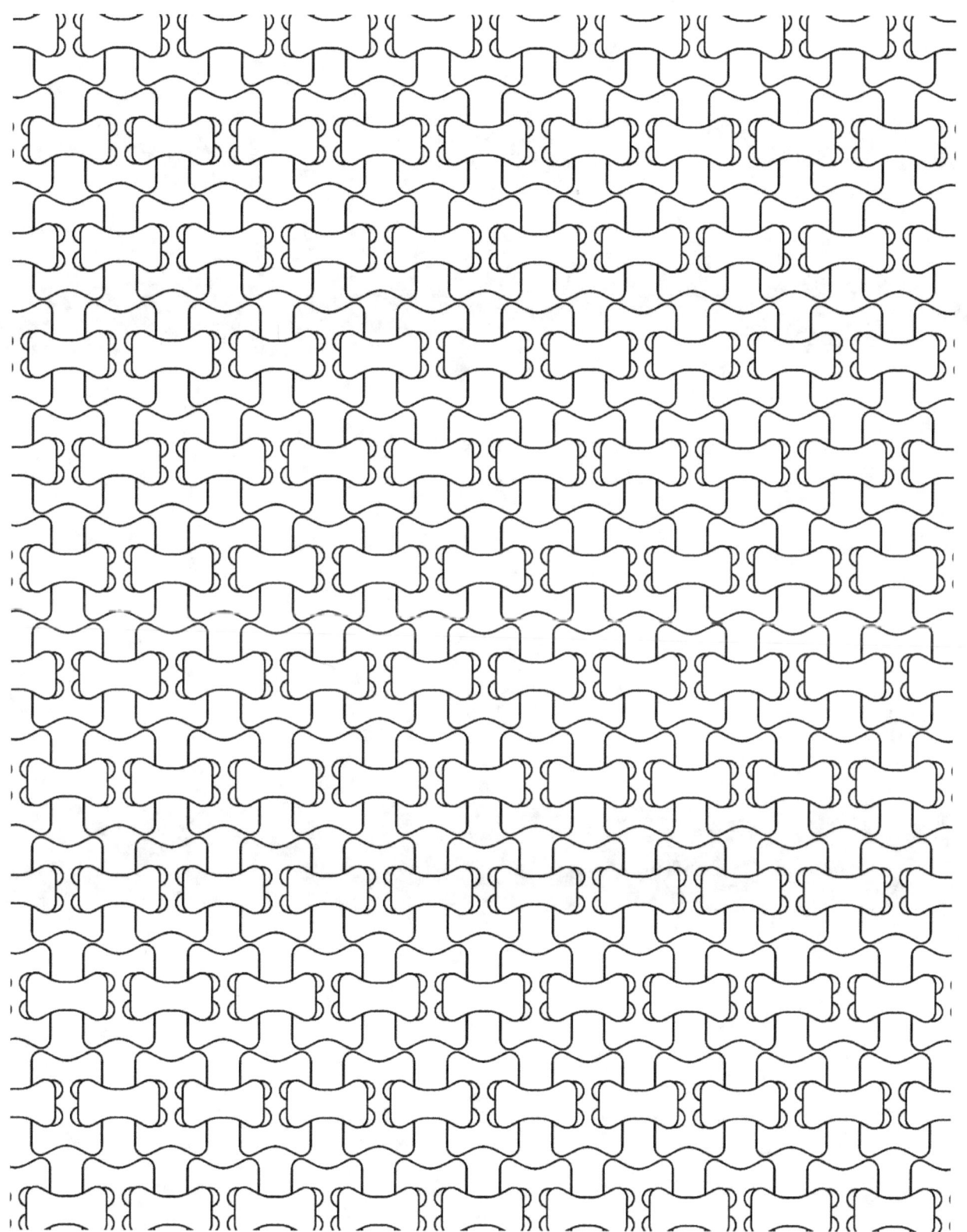

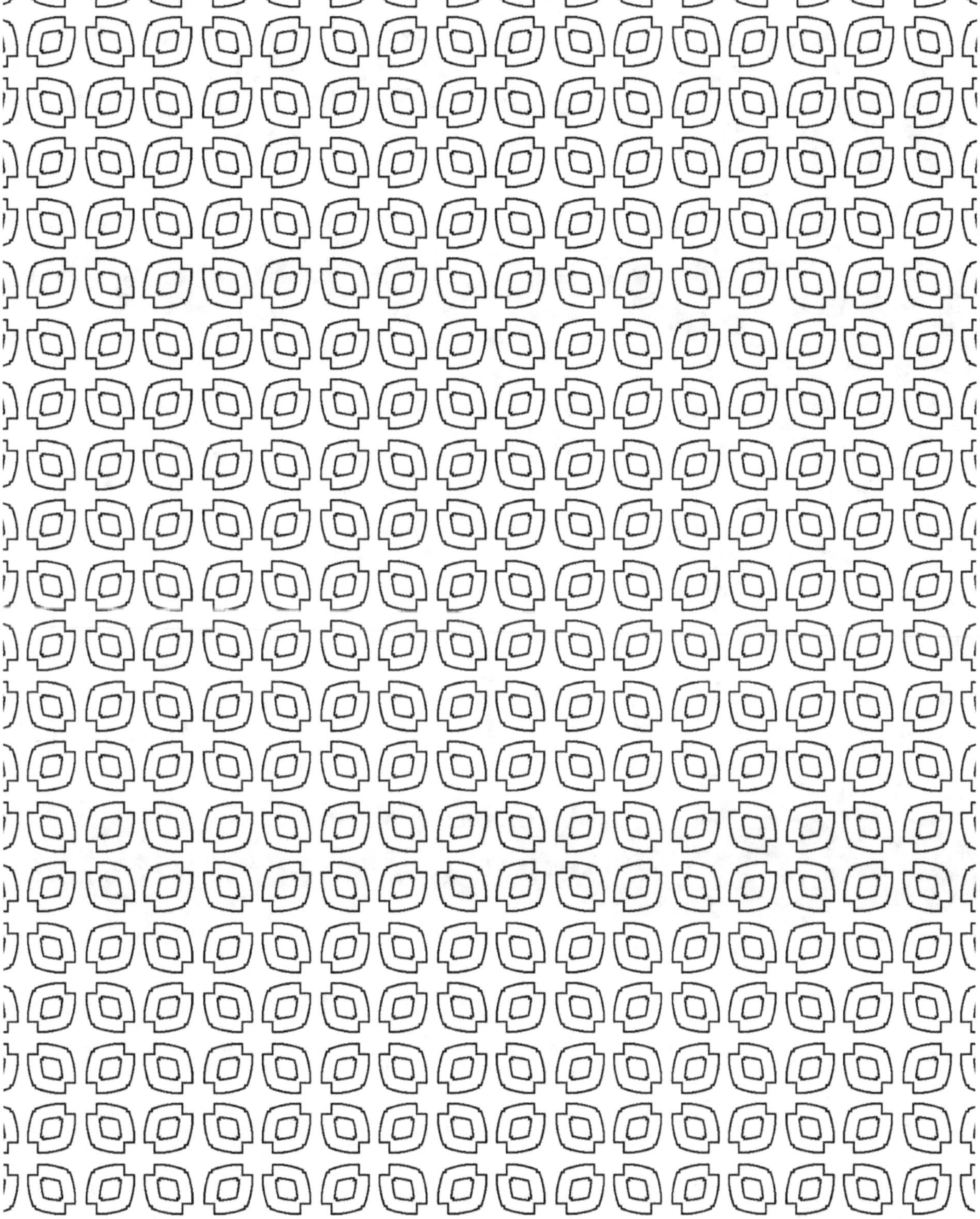

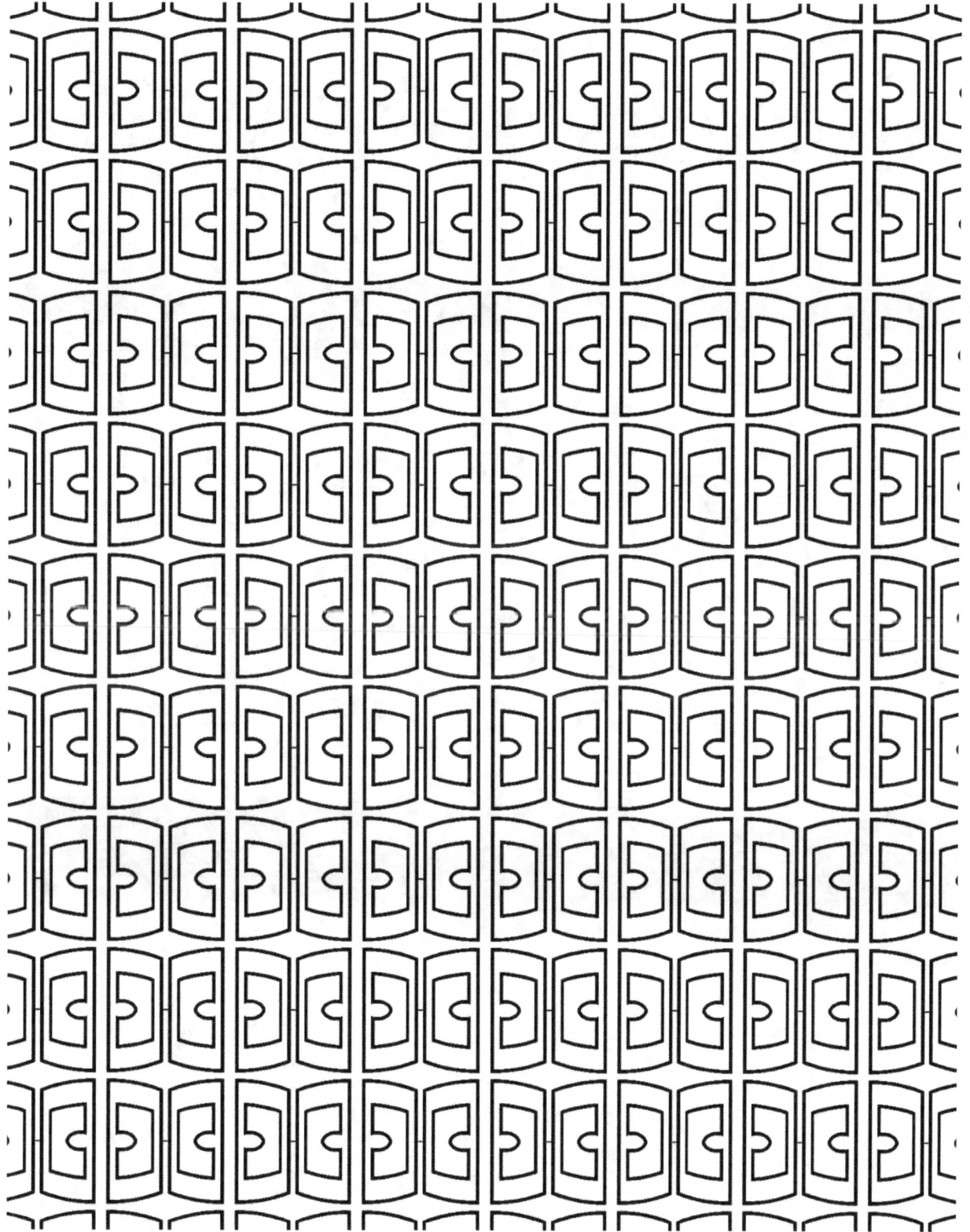

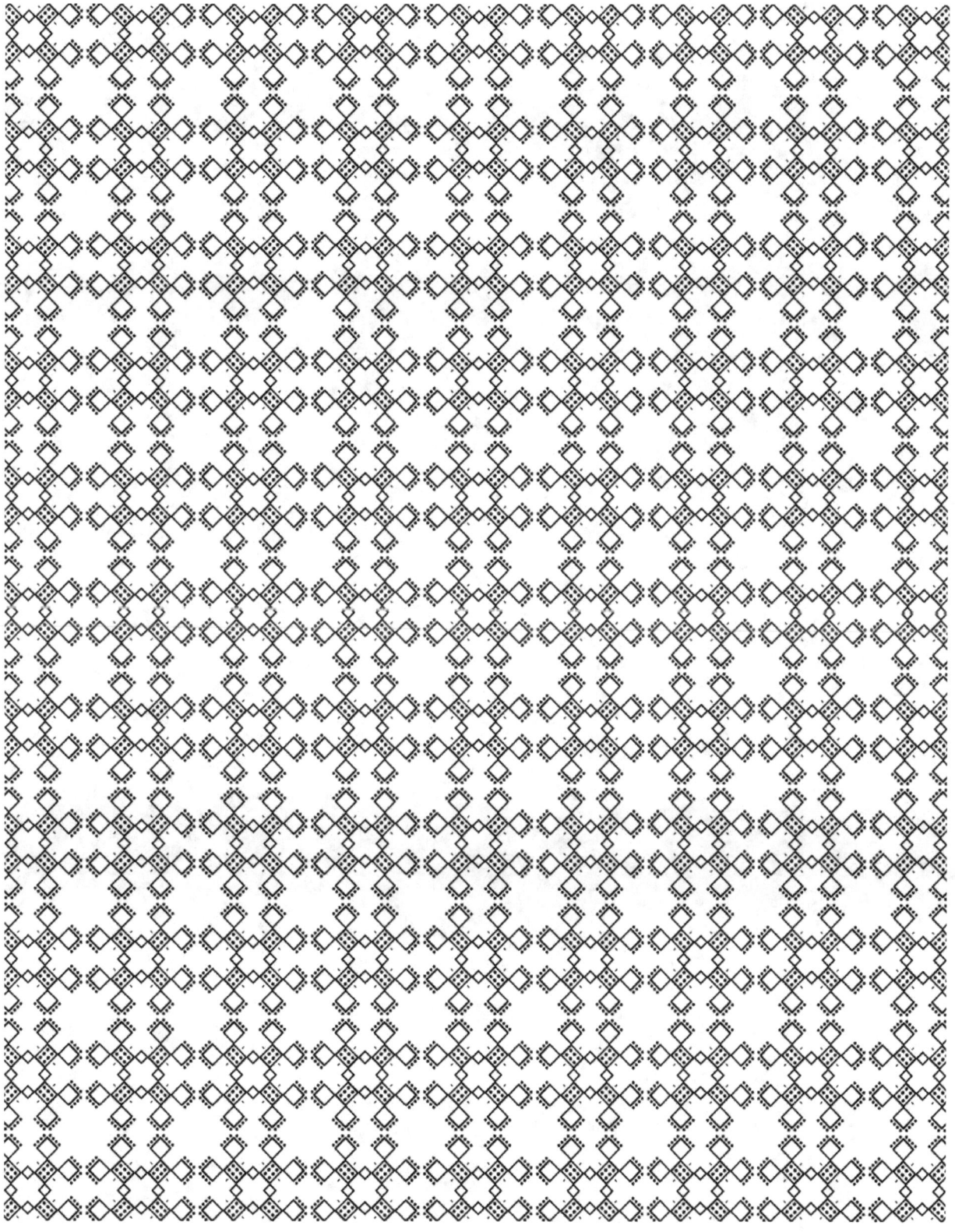

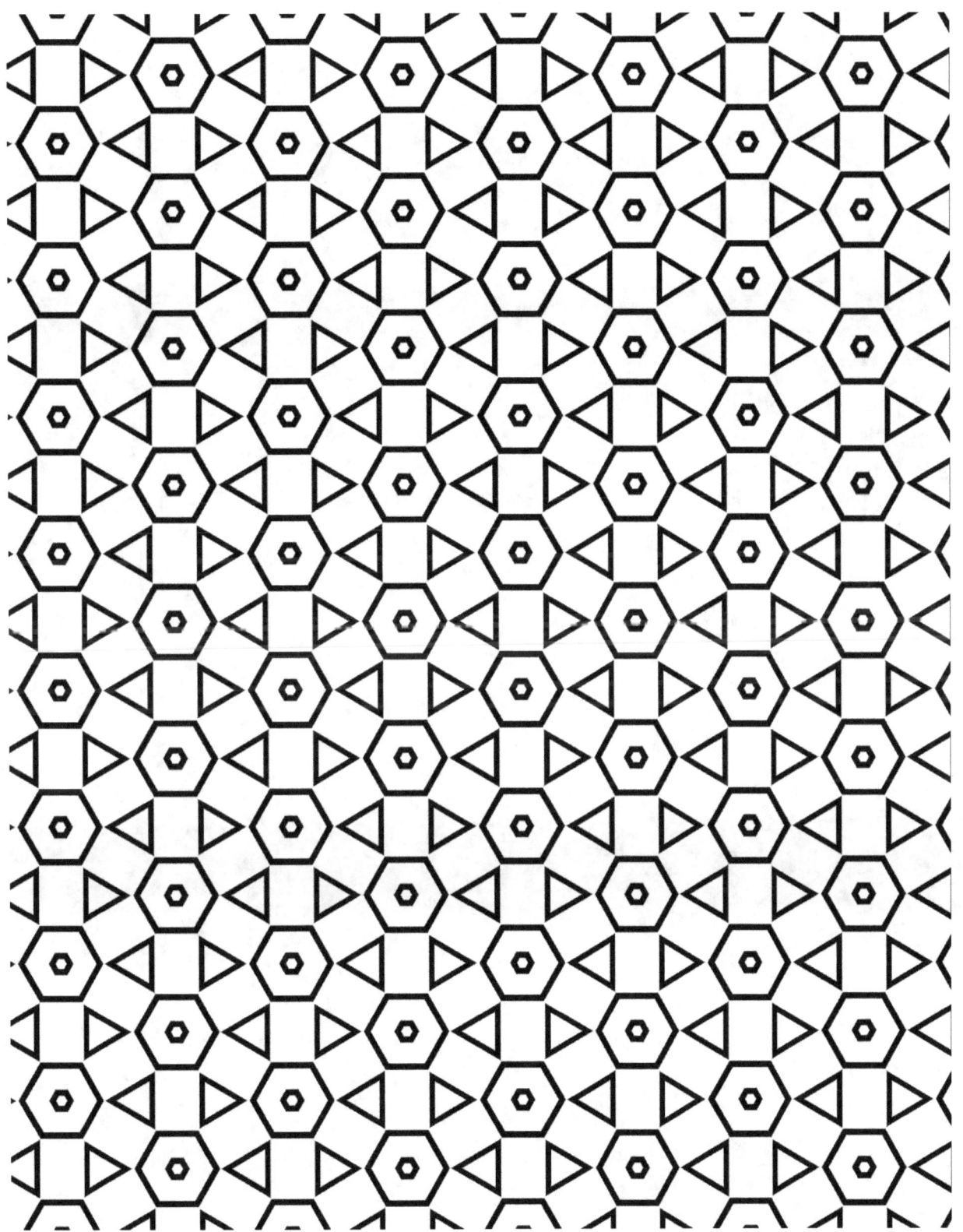

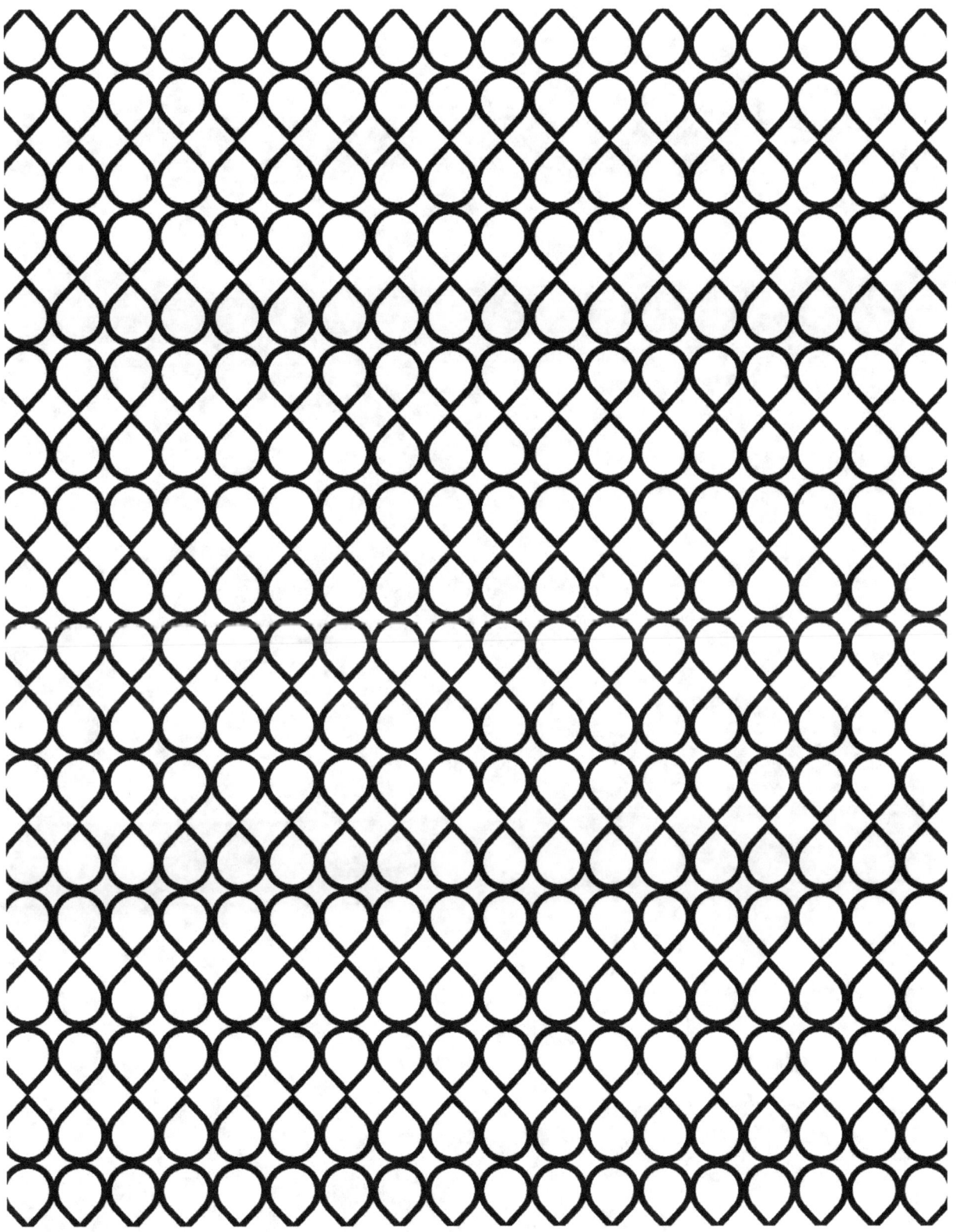

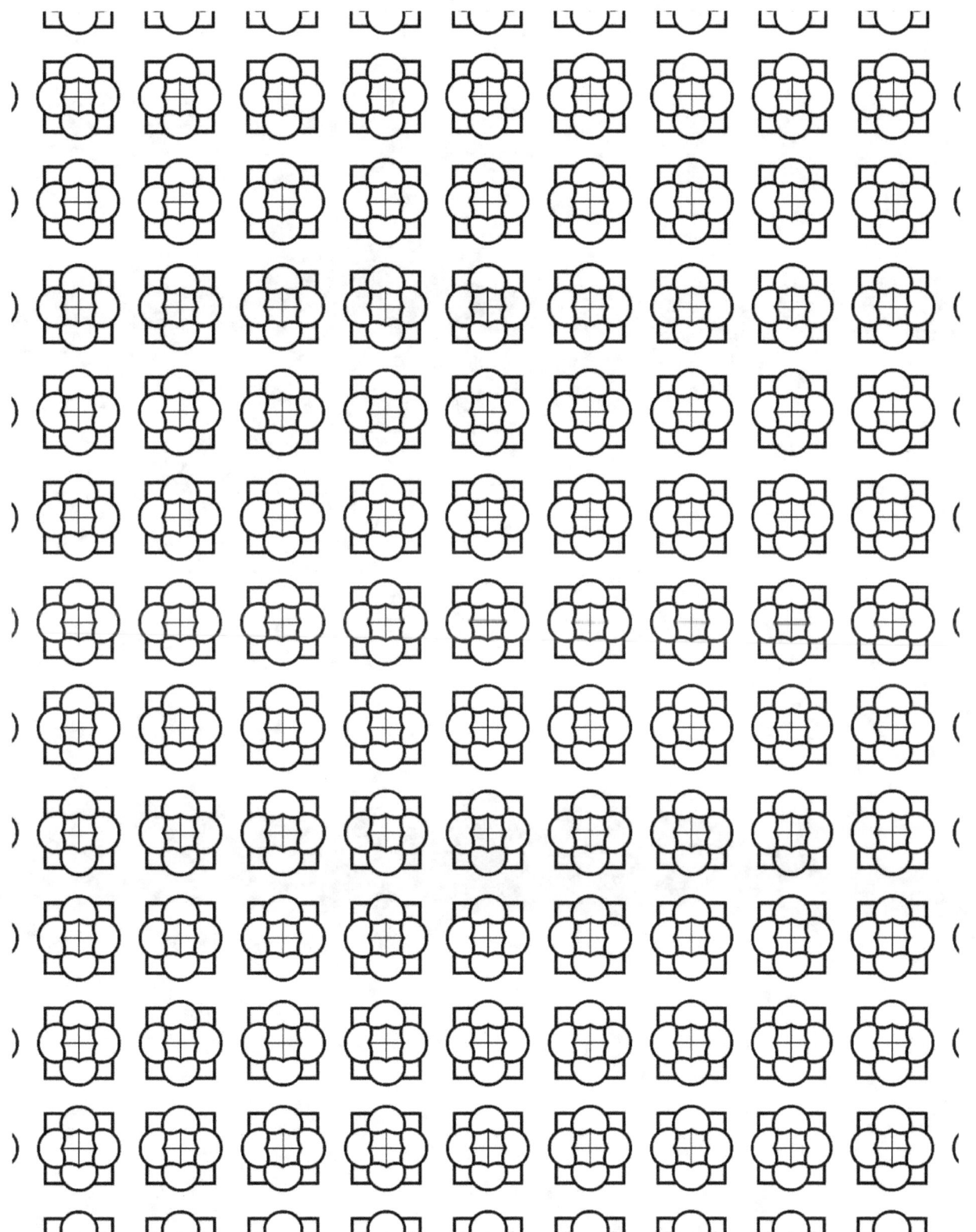

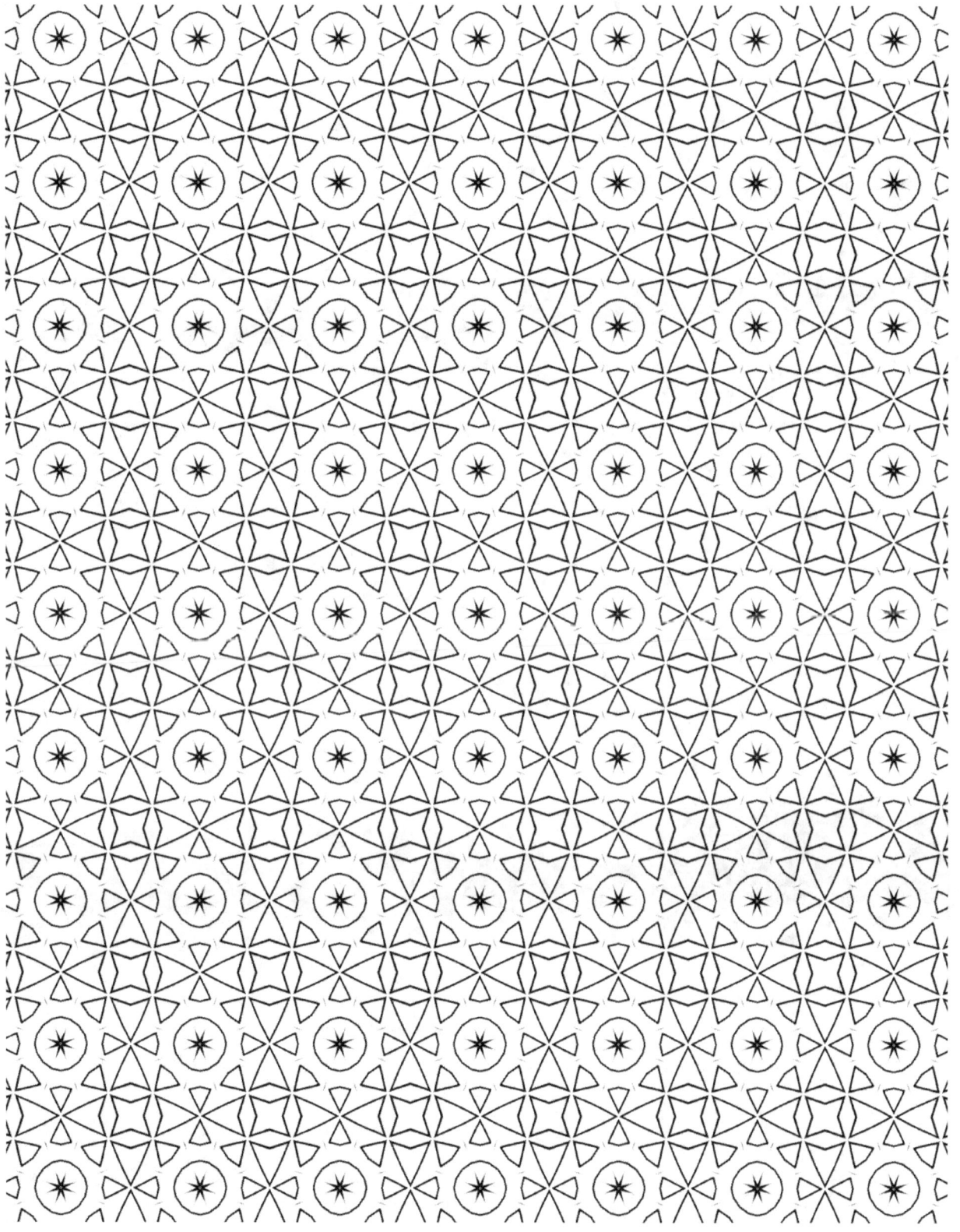

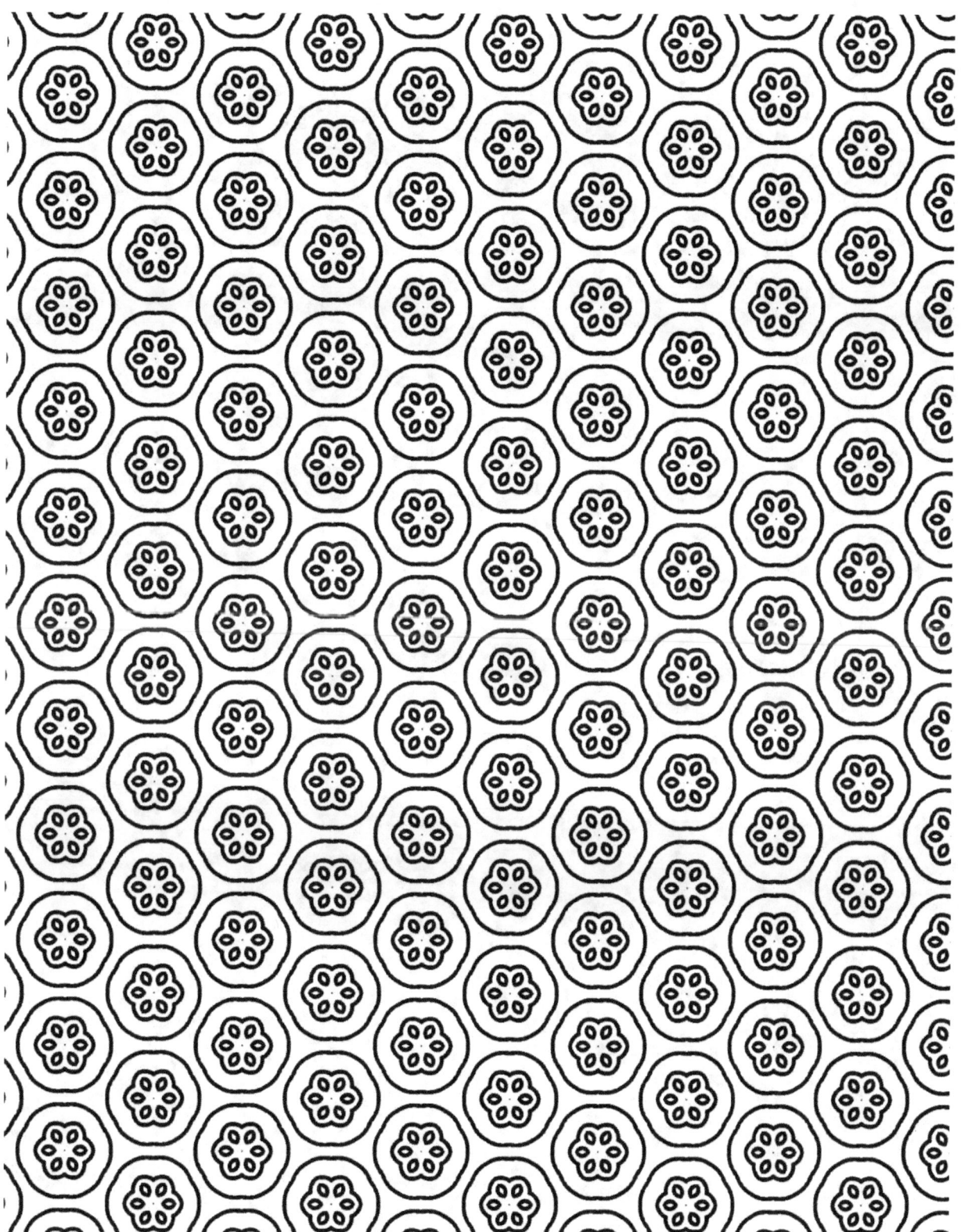

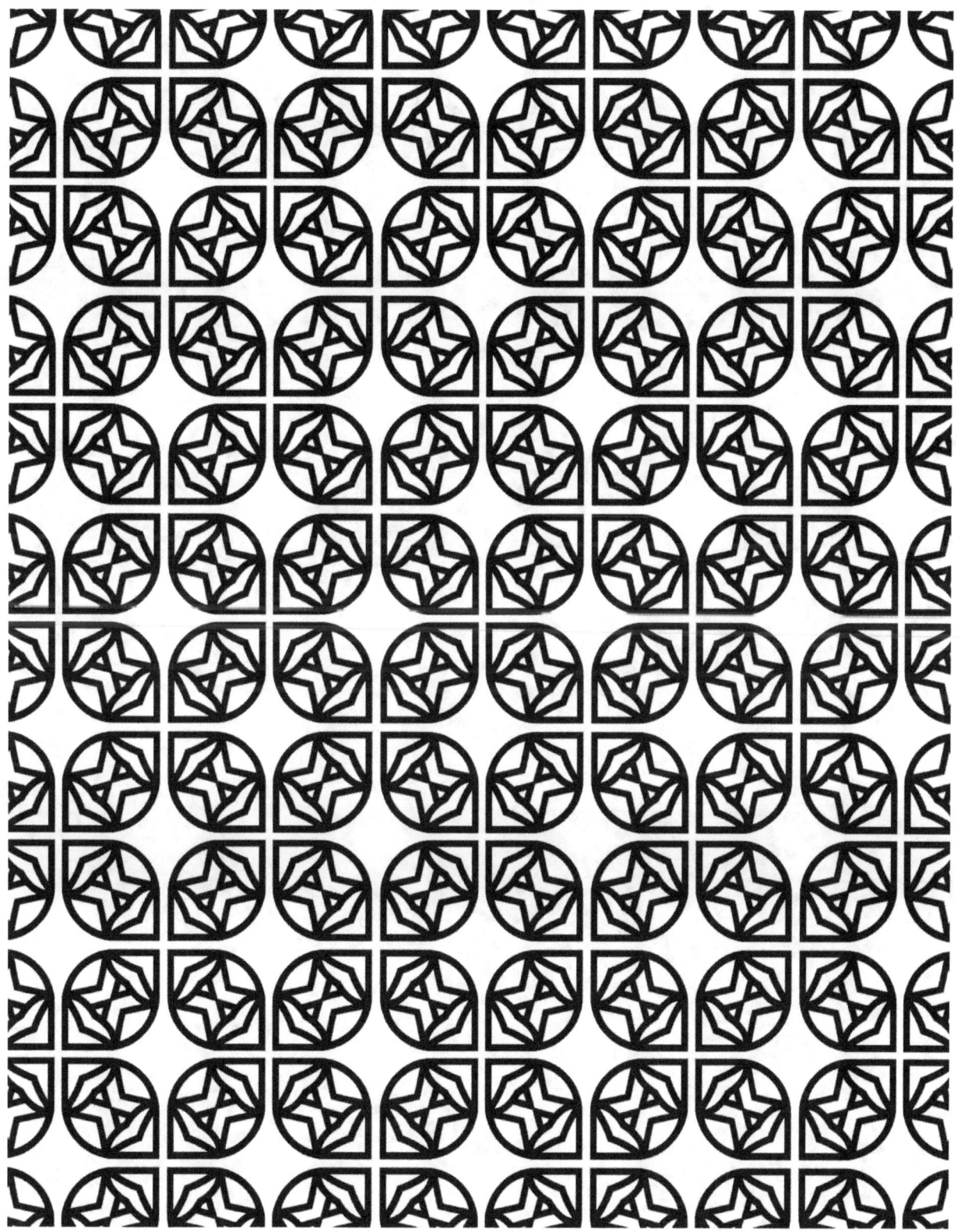

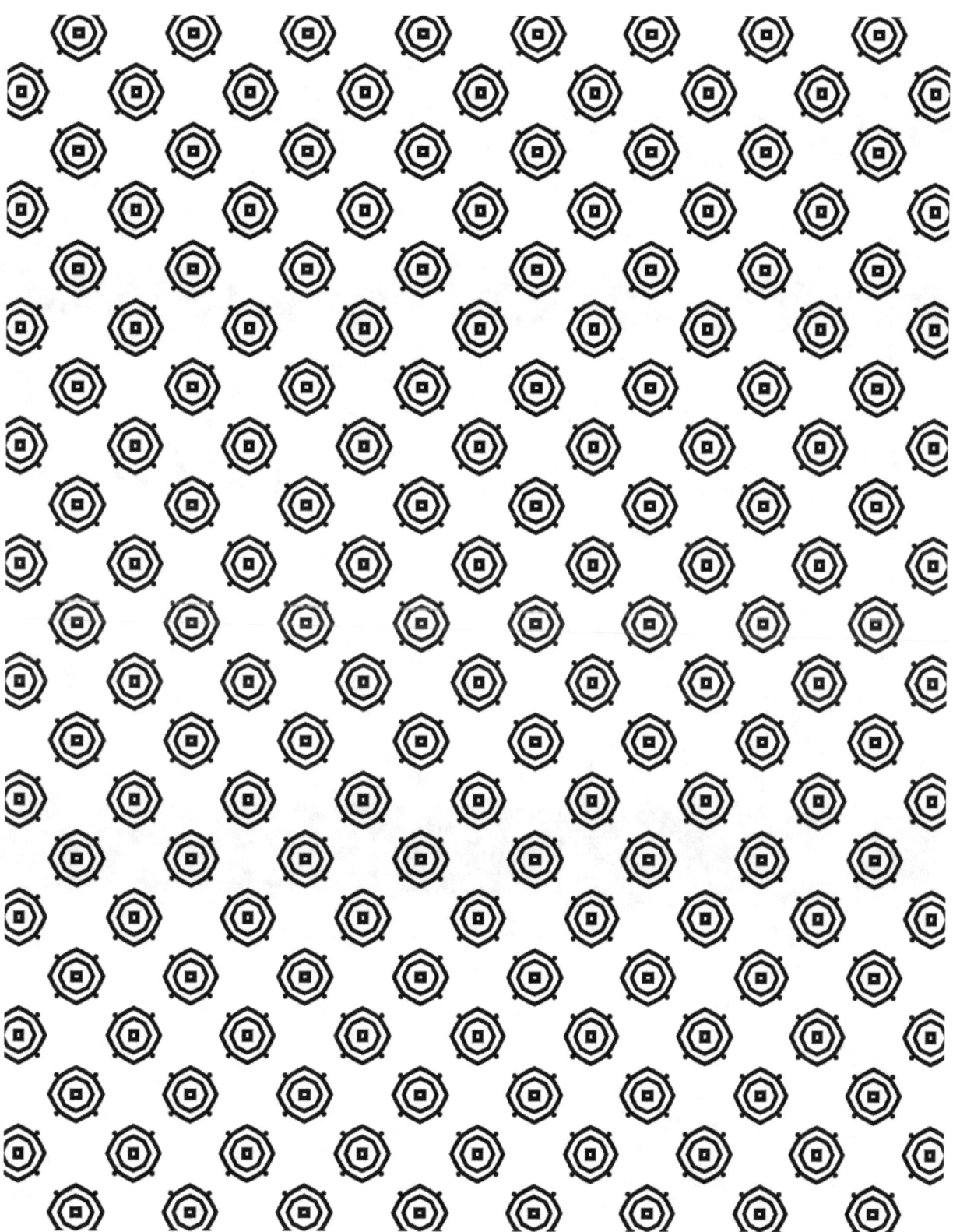

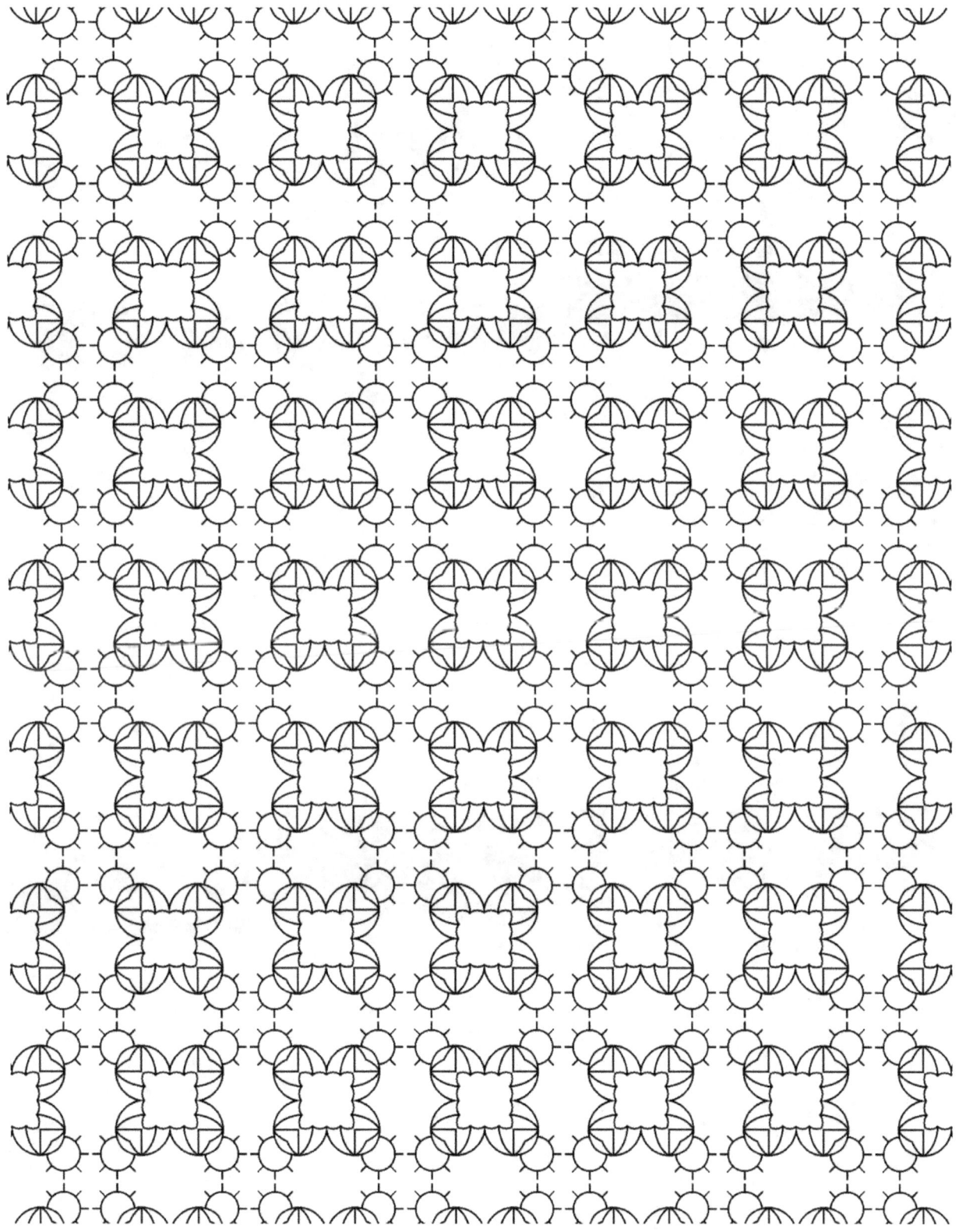

www.ingramcontent.com/pod-product-compliance
Lightning Source LLC
Chambersburg PA
CBHW081122180526
45170CB00008B/2958